COMPOST MAKES THE STRAWBERRIES GROW

****

A mother's celebration of parenting—its challenges, humor, and rewards

by

LOLITA L. JARDELEZA

RESOURCE *Publications* • Eugene, Oregon

Resource Publications
A division of Wipf and Stock Publishers
199 W 8th Ave, Suite 3
Eugene, OR 97401

Compost Makes the Strawberries Grow
A mother's celebration of parenting, its challenges, humor and rewards.
By Jardeleza, Lolita L.
Copyright © by Jardeleza, Lolita L. All rights reserved.
Softcover ISBN-13: 978-1-7252-7015-2
Hardcover ISBN-13: 978-1-7252-7017-6
eBook ISBN-13: 978-1-7252-7016-9
Publication date 2/21/2020
Previously published by Giraffe Books

With immense love and deepest gratitude

to God and Papa
who made me a mother

and to our beloved children:
Chrissy, Bim, Jack, Nini, Mecky,
Tom, Joe, Annie, Mary, Chip and Rob
who taught me eveything I know about parenting,
especially how to enjoy it

and to our beautiful children:
John, Bob, Terry, Jim, Phil
Jeannie, Theresa, Andy, Bridget and Beth
who have greatly increased the beauty in our lives.

and to their incredible children:
Charlie, Rachel, Amy, Andrew and Eddie Gallagher
Jeremiah, Elizabeth, Cody and Casey Jones
Emily, Nick, Christopher & Steve Jardeleza
Jen, Jes, Jimbo, Joshua, Katie, Jake, Joe, Rico and Jack
Hansbrough
Logan, Cody and Mac Raum
Connor, Cameron, Caleb and Justin Jardeleza
Sarah, Ben, Lisa and Matthew Jardeleza
Daniel, Colin and Liam Johnstone
LeighAnn, Blaise and Tiegan McGuire
Darby, Killian and Braeden Jardeleza
Madeleine, Libby, Billy and Luke Jardeleza
who are teaching me the fun of grandparenting!

and my beautiful grandchildren:

Sandra, Richard, Evan, Cecy, Ben, Andy, Mike, Julie, Jill, Courtney,
Chris, Miranda, Ian, Em-e, Patrick, Erica, Galex, Marcie, Taylor
C.J., Eva, and Aaron
who further increased the beauty we so enjoy!

and our magnificent great-grands:
Alex; Annabella & Marcus, Leila & Chloe, Anastasia & Elias;
Addie, Esther & Asa, Josie; Lily & Luke, Jett & Ruby, Evie;
Michaela & Will, Lolo & Jakey, Gus, Maggie, Luna, Obadiah & Finn,
Grace, Joshua, Max & Bennett, Sophia;
Gavin, Theo & Dominic; Duncan, Talia & Sonja, Maya; Harper

and beautiful great-grand—Jenna
who are the cherries on this greatgrandmother's sundae!

The Author

TABLE OF CONTENTS

ACKNOWLEDGMENTS, vii
INTRODUCTION, ix

THE BASIC PREMISES, 1

- I. Parent's Primary Function, 3
- II. The Ultimate Shortcut, 7
- III. The Gracious Cycle, 11
- IV. The Love Solution, 15
- V. Faith: The Safety Net, 21
- VI. Creative Motivation, 27
- VII. Shielding vs. Equipping, 31
- VIII. The Crucial Factor, 37
- IX. Single Parenting, 43

THE SHORTCUTS, 47

- X. Setting Priorities, 49
- XI. Basic Shortcuts, 53
- XII. Sibling Power, 57
- XIII. Fighting the Good Fight, 63
- XIV. Openness Is Freedom, 69
- XV. Listening into Being, 73
- XVI. Honestly!, 79
- XVII. Being Kind to Others, 83
- XVIII. The Pie, 87
- XIX. What about Obedience?, 93
- XX. "Mom Is Culturing Us!", 97

THE SYSTEMS, 105

- XXI. Fusion vs. Intimacy, 107
- XXII. Will They Keep Our Values?, 111
- XXIII. "As You Lie There in Smithereens"–Letting Go, 115
- XXIV. My Legacy, 119
- XXV. The Twain Shall Meet, 123
- XXVI. "Are You My Friend?", 129
- XXVII. Postscript, 133

EPILOGUE, 138

ACKNOWLEDGMENTS

I especially thank you, Papa,
for your support and
encouragement while I was writing this;

and you, Chrissy, Rob, and Neng
for lovingly editing these chapters;

and you, Bim and Nini,
for keeping after me all these years to write this book;

and especially to you, Nini,
for our many dialogues on parenthood.
You, more than any of the other children have made me think
deeply on these things.

Thank you, Chip,
for your ongoing interest and comments;

and you, Father Miguel Bernad,
for your encouragement and suggestions.

All of you were the midwives of this brainchild!

Salamat guid!

INTRODUCTION

Do you enjoy being a parent or do you find it a hassle? Do you often need a vacation from your children and wonder why?

Countless books on how to raise children are on the market and I've read my share of them. This isn't one more attempt to write still another definitive book on how to raise fine human beings or how to be a good parent. I write this book because I truly believe that *children are for enjoying*. When my children became parents, they asked me to write this book. I like to think they wanted pointers on how to enjoy their children as much as Papa and I enjoy them.

This book simply shares with you all the things that have made parenthood fun for my husband and me. Our claim to fame is that we have truly enjoyed—still enjoy—and fully expect to go on enjoying our children: those God gave us, those they married, and all of their children as well!

These days I often get the feeling that many parents consider their children nuisances, inconveniences, or at least tremendous sources of stress. The children know how their parents feel about them. This is sad because it doesn't have to be that way. Papa and I believe in our innermost beings and have proven to our satisfaction that God really meant for us to enjoy our children.

"Children are a gift from God; they are his reward" (Ps 127:3).

Thank you, God!

"In Jesus Christ who is the source of all my strength,
I have strength for everything!"

Philippians 4:13

THE BASIC PREMISES

CHAPTER 1

A PARENT'S PRIMARY FUNCTION

How would you describe a parent's primary function? Think about it and fill the blank.

A parent's primary function is: _____
_____
_____
_____

When I first became a mother I would have written something quite different from what has become my final conclusion. I arrived at that conclusion when my oldest was twenty-two—and I am a reflective person, just slow, perhaps.

At one time I thought that to be a good mother I needed to instill my own values in my children's hearts, nourish their young bodies with good, healthy meals, make sure their clothes and rooms, their hearts and minds were beautiful and clean; I also had the responsibility to provide them with those day-in, day-out things: affection, discipline, patience. All of that.

*Then one day it dawned on me
like an astronomer finding a bright new star:
a mother's primary function
is to help her children discover how wonderful they are!*

No doubt the reason it took me so long to make this discovery stemmed from the way I had been raised. I was following the pattern of my own childhood.

My mother died when I was two years old; my doting grandparents, uncles, and aunts raised me. I saw my charming father only during summer vacations, but I soon learned he had definite ideas on child-rearing. We belonged to an extended family in a culture where family is a primary value. I grew up in the era when children were supposed to be seen and not heard, and many adults had something to say about the way I was brought up.

Had I been raised in a normal family with one father and one mother, I might have raised my children differently. But so many people were contributing to my upbringing and feeding all sorts of data into my computer that it wasn't long before I was thinking, "These grown-ups don't agree on anything. They're all guessing, and my guess is as good as theirs." Without realizing it, I was picking and choosing values and techniques, philosophies and beliefs, and promising myself subconsciously that "When I have children, I'll do this or not do that." It was then that I started preparing for parenthood. I learned as much from the negative things as I did from the positive ones.

Still, when my parenting began, I used the same family tactics. I expected the same obedience and respect from my children as I had given adults: do as you are told, no mouthing whatever, never throw fits.

My family took pride in being tough. There was nothing namby-pamby or wishy-washy about them. If I was ever hurt for doing something out of line, I got the standard comment: "Merece!" ("You deserve it!") So my parenting mimicked that of my childhood. Jack knew he was not to climb on the backyard barbecue grill. When he did it anyway, fell off, and messed up his mouth, my response echoed the words of my family: "Merece!" I didn't scold in English because as a child I was not scolded in English.

In a family where everyone seemed to do everything well and seldom made mistakes, where being proper and correct were values, I stood out as the family klutz, often unacceptable. In those days, parents often used the ploy of disapproval to motivate children into modifying their behavior. So when my children came along, I tried to motivate them into better behavior with disapproval.

Then God sent me Mary Kilner. The Kilner children and ours were classmates at St. John's School. When their Chris and our Annie were a year old, they invited us to join the Teams of Our Lady with them. The Teams of Our Lady is a marriage movement for couples who wish to deepen the spiritual lives of their families. A strong friendship developed between our two families that has continued down to our grandchildren.

Mary is totally opposite from me. I envisioned my own mother to have been much like her. Never have I heard her raise her voice to any of her nine children. She seems incapable of seeing anyone's dark side. She sees people as God sees them. Mary and I had frequent conversations over the phone. Understandably, our long discussions centered on raising children. My theme song was "Toughen them up." Mary's was "Love them, love them, love them."

Mary, a cherished child, wanted to pass on the gift of cherishing to others. I, on the other hand, was a spoiled, doted-on child and, as spoiled children often end up being, not too well-liked. I was not prepared for the negative vibes of people I met. Had I been toughened up, perhaps I wouldn't have been so vulnerable.

Mary and I continued our exchange lovingly and reflectively. Father Gene Ahern, S.J., our Team chaplain, heard much about our discussions. He knew and loved our families. He commented, "You both talk as if love were the opposite of toughness and vice versa. Actually, you are talking about the two halves of a whole."

At this same time I was working on the revision of a study topic on Christian parenthood called "The Gift of Life." In my research, I came upon an article by Rachele Thomas that explained it all to my satisfaction. She said, "Love without discipline is not love. Discipline without love is not discipline." Neither works without the other. For love without discipline is only indulgence and discipline without love is plain harshness.

I was working with a couple who didn't seem to like their children very much. From this I learned that the greatest gift parents can give their children is to delight in them. I don't know why it took so long for me to arrive at this conclusion. As a child I knew what it was like to run afoul of someone.

It took another ten years for me finally to articulate this conclusion: *A mother's primary function is to help her children discover how wonderful they are!* That is much more fun than making them keep their rooms clean or eat their vegetables. When we embrace this principle, parenting shifts from *making* children be or do something to *discovering* what God has already made and to *reflecting* their own goodness back to them.

How does one do this? This is what I shall try to unfold in the following chapters. The logical statement to make at this point is: It would be easier to delight in our children and see how wonderful they are if they were not brats.

Thank you, Mary Kilner!

CHAPTER II

THE ULTIMATE SHORTCUT

In the desire of modern parents to be kind, patient, loving, and understanding, they bend over backwards to accommodate their children. I did not know I should do that. I thought it was my job to see that they grew up to be the best people they could possibly be. Consequently, I brooked no nonsense and tolerated no stupid behavior. I am amazed at how much unpleasant behavior parents tolerate in the name of love, psychology, patience, understanding, and respect for the child's freedom.

When I can hardly endure a child's unseemly behavior, I do not excuse it any more than I would excuse a grown person's rudeness nor expect anyone to put up with such behavior from me.

"But he is just a kid."

"When do you think good-mannered adults learned their good manners?"

I truly believe that children will go as far as we allow them to go. If they know that you will allow them an extra mile beyond acceptable behavior, they will go that mile. If you sit on them an inch after they've stepped past the boundary, an inch is all they'll take. As I observe the liberties parents give their children, I wonder why they allow their children that extra mile while they tear their hair out every inch of the way.

Many parents say, "It's too much trouble fighting with them." In reality, fighting is all you'll be doing if you do not set limits. But they must be definite limits. When children know you will not tolerate a particular behavior, they will not engage in it, thinking, "It's too much trouble fighting with her." I simply made sure that they got the same response from me with every single try: "No way!"

When rules are laid down early and clearly, the initial hassles may go on for a brief time, depending on the disposition of your little friend. Once the child understands, however, the efforts to cause you grief will be minimal and they will quit battering their heads against a wall that will not fall down.

Friends often asked, "Where do you get the energy and stamina to deal with the hassle?" It's simple. I don't do anything else; I reserve my energies for hassling. Today, one of our bigger hasslers says, "She was always good for a fight and was prepared to keep fighting long after you lost your stomach for it. So when you wanted something, you thought long and hard to see whether it was worth hassling for." And I always thought she hassled at the drop of a hat.

This is my capsule philosophy for raising children: Scare them out of their wits; it's efficient! When I say that, people think I'm being funny—and I am, but I also mean every word of it. When the children were small, my husband—we all call him Papa—called me "La Verduga" or in affectionate moments, "La Verdugita." That's Spanish for the executioner, feminine gender—yes, the individual in the black hood who cut off people's heads. A five-year-old daughter would scare off her tormentors by saying, "You better watch it! My mother's a witch!" When I related this to Mary Kilner, she said, "Oh, I'm so sorry." "Don't be," I said, "I count on that reputation. It simplifies my life considerably."

The secret weapon of my philosophy is a withering glare I inherited from my forebears. What the glare says is "Don't you dare!" The child's general reaction is "Oh, never mind. 'Tain't worth it." The glare stands me in better stead than my voice of authority, quick hand, forceful logic, or knowledge of psychology. It saves time, too. There's no remonstrating, arguing, fussing, frustration, and aggravation. The trick is to mean the vehemence of the glare. If you don't, the kids will know that and the glare will carry no weight.

The glare allows you to be on top of your children's behavior unobtrusively. No screaming, no hitting, no public remonstrations. Just clearing the throat to catch the culprit's attention, then flashing the glare. It is quite effective in church or with other children. It is particularly great with grandchildren. There is a silent, unequivocal understanding between them and you. There is no verbal abuse, no psychological attack, no physical contact or mental anguish. It says nothing that could undermine a child's self-confidence nor is it threatening. The child's imagination is your best ally. There is no rejection, no dismissal, no scathing judgment. The glare just stops them in their tracks.

The glare says enough to be undeniable but is so ambiguous that they don't know what to do about it nor do they recognize options. They don't know your rules but they cannot deny your unmistakable, unassailable anger, disapproval, or displeasure.

When corrected, most children basically understand the unspoken "I love you too much to let you be a brat." First, I explain why the behavior is inappropriate in firm, friendly terms the child can understand. If he needs a second explanation, I oblige—firmly. The glare accompanies the third explanation. End of story. It is a great shortcut.

Does this sound easy? Does the glare produce instant good behavior? It works for me. What happens when you're not a glarer by temperament or natural equipment? My gentle, kindhearted daughter-in-law, Terry, practices in front of a mirror. She has seen how it works for her husband—my son Jack—who has inherited it from his forebears.

How does one learn to glare? First, it has to come from real, genuine displeasure on the part of the glarer unless you are a consummate actor or actress. If you think the child's antics really are cute, the glare won't glare. Secondly, you clench your jaw and grit your teeth as if you could chew metal or devour humans. Finally, bug out your eyes and let them flash fire.

Shakespeare puts it well:

> ... imitate the action of the tiger:
> Stiffen the sinews, summon up the blood,
> Disguise fair nature with hard-favour'd rage;
> Then lend the eye a terrible aspect;
> Let it pry through the portage of the head
> Like the brass cannon; let the brow o'erwhelm it
> As fearfully as doth a galled rock
> O'erhang and jutty his confounded base,
> Swill'd with the wild and wasteful ocean.
> Now set the teeth and stretch the nostril wide;
> Hold hard the breath, and bend up every spirit
> To his full height.
>
> *King Henry V*, Act III, Scene I

Once you firmly establish the fact that you will not tolerate unacceptable behavior, the children will behave better more frequently and consistently. As my second daughter Bim puts it, "There are no bad children for Mom." (Actually my saying is: there are no bad children, only hungry and/or sleepy ones.)

I didn't need vacations from my children. When they behave well you enjoy them more. The more you enjoy them, the more they see that you delight in them. The more they see this, the better they feel about themselves. The better they feel about themselves, the nicer they are. The nicer they are, the more you enjoy them. The gracious cycle is on!

Thank you, Forebears!

CHAPTER III

THE GRACIOUS CYCLE

We had not seen little Marcy in a while so it was a joy to see her and her mother. "Hi, Marcy! We haven't seen you in such a long time!" "Aw, shaddap!" she responded. I said nothing to correct the behavior since it was her mother's place to do that, not mine. We sat down and began catching up on each other's news. Marcy wandered into the kitchen. "Would you like some milk and cookies?" I asked. "Aw, shaddap!" she responded again. Still there was no comment from her mother. I gave the child milk and cookies, and when she finished eating I asked, "Would you like some more?" "Aw, sh—" she began. At this point, I said to her quietly and evenly, "Don't you talk to me that way. I welcomed you and was glad to see you; I offered you goodies and I don't see how you get off talking to me like that. I don't allow my children to talk to me that way and I won't allow it from you either. Do you understand?"

Marcy understood and discarded her bad manners for the rest of her visit. At that point her mother said, "I belong to the school of thought that maintains that if you let children alone, they will eventually learn good manners by themselves."

"In the meantime," I responded, "they haven't gotten the hang of it yet, and they'll be picking up negative vibes about themselves from people they meet. By the time they get around to acquiring good manners, they will have been convinced that people don't like them. Such a pity. One of the gifts we can give our children is to help them learn to behave in ways that show consideration for others so that wherever they go people will give them good vibes about themselves.

In parent-child relationships, there is one of two cycles operating: one vicious, the other gracious. The first one goes like this: Parents give their children a lot of leeway to behave as they please. The fewer the limits children have, the brattier they tend to be. The brattier they are, the less their parents like them. The less parents like their children, the guiltier they feel. The guiltier they feel, the more leeway they give the children. The more leeway the children get, the more liberties they take. The more liberties they take, the brattier they become. The brattier they are, the less their parents like them. The vicious cycle is locked in place.

Jane and Dave do not want to suppress their children. When they ask their children to do something and the child demurs, they "respect" the child's wishes.

"Kathy, it's time to take a nap."

"I don't want to take a nap."

"You'll get very tired if you don't."

"I don't want to take a nap!"

"All right, Dear."

Nearing suppertime, four-year-old Kathy is tired and cross. She whines, demands a lot of attention, and is sassy.

In the meantime, another dialogue is going on.

"Gary," says Jane, "will you help me get dinner ready? Please set the table while I take care of Kathy."

"Aw, Mom, I'm watching TV!"

Now, Jane must contend with cranky Kathy while she tries to get dinner on the table. She is irritated with Kathy and Gary and she feels guilty. When both come to the table and say, "Meatloaf again? Yuck!" Jane says nothing, but she likes them even less and feels even more guilty. "A mother shouldn't have such negative feelings about her own children," she thinks.

The after-dinner scenario goes like this: "Gary, could you clear the table while I get Kathy ready for bed?"

"Mom, leave me alone!" Gary yells while Kathy goes upstairs wailing, "I don't want to go to bed!"

Jane isn't enjoying any of this. She feels guiltier than ever because her kids are brats. She reasons, "How can I feel this way about my own children? I have to be more loving toward them. I mustn't be harsh. I have to be patient." Meanwhile, Gary and Kathy wonder if their mother really likes them. She seems to cringe when they approach her.

Here is a second scene. The parents lay down the ground rules early. They are clear, loving, and firm. The children want to please as children do, so they keep their end of the bargain. The better they behave, the more their parents enjoy them. The more their parents delight in them, the more affirmed they feel. The better they feel about themselves, the happier they are. The happier they are, the better they behave. The better they behave, the more their parents affirm them. This is the gracious cycle.

Chuck, who is five, comes in after lunch with his friend, Jay. "Mom, Jay wants me to stay at his house for the rest of the afternoon. May I?"

"Aren't you planning to see the play tonight?"

"Oh, yeah!"

"Wouldn't it be better to take a nap so you won't be so tired tonight? The play doesn't end until eleven."

"Oh, okay! Sorry, Jay."

Jay's father, looking on says, "What an incredible kid! Wish he were mine!" Mother feels a warm glow and puts her arm around Chuck as they go upstairs. Chuck feels these positive vibes and gets a sense of well-being.

After his nap, Mother asks Chuck to set the table. "We're eating early tonight, and I have to bathe the little girls."

"But, Mom, I want to watch TV."

"I know, Dear, but I'm pressed for time and I need your help. It doesn't take that long."

"Okay, Mom."

At dinner, Mom says, "Dad, Chuck was such a help to me" and goes on to tell the family what Jay's father had said. Dad affirms the boy and he feels appreciated. Mom thinks Chuck is a good child and it's evident from the way she looks at him and touches him. Chuck can't miss it in the tone of her voice and the look in her eyes.

Many young mothers are reluctant to correct their children because they don't want them to feel bad. So the children continue their bad behavior eliciting bad vibes from people around them. That makes them feel good?

When does the cycle begin? At birth. A child picks up affirmation or a lack of it not only from what is said. Communication is much more than words. Vibes, body language, and looks communicate strongly. The tone of voice and cadences with which we speak may belie what we are saying. A stern message in a cooing tone or a sweet message in a stern tone will confuse the child. If the parents' general message is, "You are wonderful!" the child absorbs that through his pores. If the message is "You are such a nuisance!" the same thing happens.

Toni Fisher lived across from us when the children were quite small. She was one of ten children from a warm, happy home, and her stories about her volatile mother gave me hope when I felt bad about myself as a mother. Toni was the kind of woman I wanted my daughters and me to become. If anyone needed help, Toni and/or her husband, Leo, would turn up at the doorstep. When our Tom got second degree burns on his back from scalding coffee, I came down with the flu. Leo came to the door with lunch; when he realized how much we needed help, he returned with Toni and the two of them gifted us with order and cleanliness, hearty meals, good cheer, and the healing we needed.

When life became too difficult, I would go across the street to see Toni and "desahogar" (undrown) myself. The English term is "unburden" but the Spanish "desahogar" is more fitting. She would listen to me and make mother hen noises but would never give advice nor take sides. I'd return home feeling much better. She knew I was frustrated with our garden. It needed so much care and always looked like a jungle. But unbeknownst to me, she took roses and mountain laurel and entered them in her garden club's show. Imagine the charge I got when they won ribbons!

She knew that I rated myself a poor mother because I was often angry and upset, disorganized, and perpetually out of kilter. She once said to me, "When you truly love your children, you can yell and smack and rage, but they'll feel loved. When you don't love them, you can try to hide that with gifts and indulgence, but they'll know you don't." Love cannot be disguised.

It was Toni's loving reassurance that helped me discover I was okay, that I could go on with confidence in my ability to mother well. One reason many parents have a difficult time parenting today is their lack of confidence in themselves. We look for techniques, special systems, and philosophies, but we don't really have to. Like the bluebird, the answers are in our own backyard: love, logic, and common sense. My being able to trust that my love would see me through my inadequacies allowed me to begin enjoying parenthood.

Thank you, Toni and Leo Fisher!

CHAPTER IV

THE LOVE SOLUTION

My basic premise for fun parenting is love. Love makes us see the wonders in our children so that we can help them discover them, too. Love prompts us to help our children behave so they'll know themselves to be lovable. Love helps us discover all the different creative ways they can uncover their most loving and lovable selves. Love will give them everything they need to embrace life. Love is the bond in family life where we trust they will thrive, blossom, and bloom. Love for them sets our priorities. Love is the basis for all the commonsense practices that make our day-to-day interaction a little smoother. Not altogether smooth—just a little smoother.

In my experience, love is precisely not a smooth-sailing affair. Love often means putting the other before self; it is difficult because it means dying to self. On the other hand, catering to one's own self-will is equally difficult because selfishness is as addictive and destructive as cocaine. Since both are going to hurt, it is wise to go with the constructive; namely, love. Love builds and increases, releases and strengthens, beautifies and elates.

Every relationship involving two different personalities means give and take, misunderstanding and understanding, hurting and healing, adjusting and readjusting. A household of thirteen like ours involves numerous different relationships.

If people knew that at least one person loved them unconditionally, that would be enough to see them through whatever life had in store for them. Just one person. For me, that was Nanay, my paternal grandmother who raised me. Even if I was dubious, I had no doubts that Nanay truly cherished me. I also knew she delighted in me. Are our children certain we cherish them? Do they know we delight in them?

Our first task is to soak our children in a saturated solution of love the first three years of their lives and they will feel loved for as long as they live.

What is a "saturated solution of love"?

To me this means meeting the child's needs. Is she hungry? Feed her. Is he sleepy? Put him to sleep. If he wants to be rocked, rock him. If she wants a story, read to her. Does she want to be held? Hold her. If they want a song, sing to them. Does he want to talk? Listen to him. Do whatever you can to make him understand that you are for him. When Bim proofread the first draft of these chapters, she said, "Mom, be sure you mention that you would lie down with us at naptime and sing to us and tell us stories. You mention your 'fits' but you left that out."

Some children are more clingy than others. In Visayan, the particular Filipino language we speak, our term for such children is "omang." An omang will cling to his mother, cry when she leaves the room, get frantic when he can't find her. In short, he wants to be an appendage of her. I had some like that; I think they are born that way. So I went along. I held them and carried them on my back while I did the housework, took them with me if I could. Somewhat ironically, they have grown up to become my most independent children.

Fortunately, I was raised in a culture where this was done. There was no fear that we would spoil the baby if we catered to his needs. It was the logical thing to do. But that was possible because we had servants who tended to the house while the mothers tended to the baby or vice versa. Over the years, I've lived as if I had servants. I just don't have them, that's all.

What about the housework?

Housework will go undone, especially if your child is anxious or colicky or high-strung. If you have more than one child, the chaos could go on for what seems an interminable length of time. Mine went on for about eighteen years. By that time, this way of life was the norm for me. Soaking with love went on for eighteen years; the chaos went on much longer. Adventure is high on my list of priorities, and facing chaos every morning gives me my daily dose of adventure!

Many of my close friends also have many children who are well-mannered, but they do not live in chaos. Perhaps you don't either. That chaotic way of being flows, I believe, from my own erratic temperament. Consequently, I am a sign of hope to many harassed women. They see me go from one error to another and yet have children I enjoy. I am living proof that God takes care of his little idiots.

But what about the housework? I stayed in bed with the children only when I was reading a good book. I'd sing the song each child requested with the proviso that when all the songs were sung, I would tend to the house and they would take their naps. If they couldn't fall asleep, they could just lie there and "think pretty thoughts" which put them to sleep.

How can you give each child the love and attention he or she needs when there are several of them?

Emilia commented on that. She said, "The more children you have, the more you must divide yourself and the less of you they get." But I asked, "If I had only two, which half of me would Chrissy get? the top half or the bottom half, my left half or my right half? The reality is, I'm like Sam Levenson's mother: the wall-to-wall type."

One way out is to work with the children. Little ones love to "work" and this is a good time to teach them. It was a big, merry, messy game for us! But I got to the task. I taught them, paid attention to them, and everyone had a ball. This was possible for me because I'm not a perfectionist; I believe in using all teachable moments. A perfectionist would find this difficult.

It would have been easier to keep a clean kitchen if I had done all the cooking. But I trained a different cook for every day of the week, and that was something else. The other side of the coin, however, was that they could prepare entire meals, bake goodies, and make bread before they were teenagers.

Is love always a matter of time and space? How do you know someone loves you? Is it because he or she is around you as often as possible? I like having the people who love me around a lot, but I still feel they love me even if they aren't around.

Love is a perspective. People who love us focus on our beautiful side. They may see our dark side and even point it out to us, but they treat us as if we had none. They also tell us in words, in gestures, in gifts, in the way they look at us or touch us, in the way they speak about us to others, the way they seek us out. Won't our children feel loved if they experience these same actions?

Matt is almost too easygoing. Unmotivated is the word he uses. Love's perspective dwells on Matt's fun-loving, easy-to-get-along-with, laid back personality. Frank, however, has a short fuse and becomes easily exasperated. Love's perspective concentrates on his ability to achieve, his precision, and his willingness to work hard to reach his goals. When you change a diaper, it's amazing what a difference it makes whether you focus on the baby or on the diaper. Love's perspective means focusing on the baby, talking to her, making her laugh, getting her to gurgle and coo, nuzzling her. Love's perspective allows us to enjoy the child.

One saturating-in-love way is to get across to the children how marvelous you think they are. One of my favorite statements was: "I'm so glad God gave you to me. He could have given you to Mrs. Kilner, but he didn't. He gave you to me!" When they were being difficult, I'd tell them, "It's a good thing I love you." Often, at the height of a shouting match, I'd throw in, "If you ever wondered whether I love you or not, believe that I do, because if I didn't, I would have given up a long time ago."

Nick Curtin once remarked that we were the most tactile family he knew. We like hugs and kisses; what the kids call "lovins and huggins." They go a long, long way and, like the glare, they communicate volumes. When I have no solution for another's pain, I simply hug her.

We also write love letters to one another. I was the mushy sort, putting love notes in my husband's lunch box. As the children learned to read, I'd leave love notes on their dressers, write them love poems for Valentine's Day, thank-you notes on Mother's Day. They began writing us love notes when they learned to write. One day, I discovered that they also wrote love notes to each other.

A game we enjoyed playing was called LIFT. We took thirteen small index cards and wrote the person's name in the upper left-hand corner. Below that name, we listed everyone else's name. Next to our names we wrote what we thought was the nicest thing about the person whose name was in the upper left-hand corner. When the card completed the rounds you got to keep it—a reminder of the things the family liked about you.

What astonished me about this game was that more gratifying than knowing how much the others like you was discovering how much you liked the others! In all this, we discovered that affirmation and affection, admiration and appreciation can be habit-forming and can improve life considerably!

Did your children always feel you loved them?

I hope so, but I can't believe they always did. I've done things psychologists say emotionally cripple children for life. But I guess the children just didn't take me seriously. One of their favorite pastimes is to gather after a holiday meal and reminisce about me as if I weren't there, laughing themselves silly. "Remember when she would throw the mattresses out the window when we didn't make our beds and we'd find them out on the driveway when we got home from school?" Hoot. Howl. Roar. "And how about the time she...."

Finally, I asked them directly, "Why didn't you hold my nastiness and meanness against me?" Joe answered, "You didn't fool us. We always knew how much you loved us!" Toni Fisher was right. Praise God!

Am I ever glad God gave you to me! Thank you, guys!
Thank you, Nanay!

CHAPTER V

FAITH: THE SAFETY NET

As fortunate and felicitous as my findings on parenting have been over the years, I believe that God is the real reason for our joy in parenting.

When I was expecting Chip, I had taken prednisone during the first trimester, unaware that it could cause deformity in a fetus. Truly shaken, I went to Father Paul Bechard seeking peace and strength.

"Father, life is like walking on a tightrope. I'm always afraid of falling."

"That's all right, Dear," he said. "When you fall, you fall into the hands of God."

That's the neat thing about God; he is our safety net. I'm not sure we all realize that. If we did, we wouldn't be so uptight about parenting. We worry because we are aware of our inadequacies and how they can affect our children. Actually, inadequacies can be an advantage.

I was a child who often heard the comment, "Do you suppose she'll ever amount to anything?" I was the girl with the college boyfriend who said, "Of all the girls we guys knew, she was the one we voted as the one we least wanted to marry." When you get feedback like that, you learn something very quickly: "Lord, no one needs you more than I."

Awareness of my many limitations early in life taught me to depend on God for absolutely everything. When the children came one after the other, I looked for help wherever I could find it. Marge Geist belonged to the Legion of Mary with Toni and me. She had two lovely children, Jon and Jan. She shared this formula for parenting with me and I found it helpful:

Read, observe, reflect.
Try your hardest, do your best.
Entrust them to Mary, mother of Jesus.
Relax. (This was the hardest.)

When our Carmelite cousin, Father Bernard, baptized Jack, he asked Mary to care for Jack just as she had cared for her son, Jesus. Other priests made the same prayer for some of our subsequent children. In 1965, we took all those who had not been placed in Mary's care to the Carmelite chapel and formally entrusted them to her. We have also done this with all of the grandchildren.

I asked Mary to make up for all my mistakes and omissions, and I made so many I maintain that our children are such joys because Mary raised them! The Lord, too, bridges the gap between the love I give my children and the love they need from me. God is, indeed, our safety net. He fills the holes of my inadequacies with his own Spirit.

We ask the Lord to be Lord of our family and he takes over from there. Often, when I suggest this prayer to others, they say "I've turned everything over to him," or "I've asked him to be in charge." It's not the same, for we can turn things over to janitors or ask them to be in charge. "Being Lord of" is much more.

When we ask the Lord to be Lord, it is important to release whatever that is to his lordship. Often, we ask him to be Lord and then proceed to dictate what we want him to do as if he were our lackey. Why do we do this? He does a good job without our coaching. Once I asked a friend, "If you have prayed about this, why do you worry? Do you think God won't do a good job?" "That's right," she responded. "He always makes a mess of things!" I hadn't noticed.

Parenting has driven me to prayer. When I started on the job, I felt confused, bewildered, and rather helpless. How does one juggle all the factors that go into parenting and all the tasks that comprise parenting without the help of God? Personally, I don't know. I pray because I have a dire need to understand what God wants of me as person, wife, and mother.

I told Father Bob McCreary, my spiritual director, that I didn't know how to pray. He suggested I take each member of the family before the Lord and tell him the needs of each and my concerns for each. This has helped me understand God's will for my children because this kind of praying allows me to listen to God's will for them.

When Tom was sixteen, he said to me, "Why are you pegging your life on God and praying? My friends' mothers don't and they're nicer than you. Mrs. Parker's thing is glamour and Mrs. Mercer's is sports, but they are kinder than you."

"Tom, that's because Mrs. Parker and Mrs. Mercer are naturally good, kind people. Do you realize that if I didn't peg my life on God and didn't pray, I'd be my natural self?"

"What's that?" he asked.

"Mean as hell and lazy as sin."

The next day, Tom came home and found me in a bolt-crunching rage while I was scrubbing the floors.

"Come here," I snarled. "D'you see this? This is my natural self!"

He bent down, touched me gently on the shoulder and said, "Pray, Mama, pray!"

If I could give my children only one gift, without hesitation it would be a love for God. As in kindness, all else would follow the love of God: love for neighbor, acceptance of self, peace, justice, humility, integrity, joy, strength.

Can we teach love of God?

Mary Reed Newland's books on raising children were my old standbys. She stated that when you overtly love your children, tell them there is someone who loves them more than you do. They'll say it's their other parent. Tell them, "Even more than that." Then tell them that it's God. A personal experience of love helps to convince us that God loves us so much.

As I dried my very little children after their baths, I'd say, "Thank you, God, for Chrissy's hair. Thank you, God, for Chrissy's eyes," and on until they were dry. I wanted them to be aware of God's presence. When Joe was about two, I put him in his crib and said, "Say goodnight to God, Joe." Turning to the crucifix near his crib, he flexed his baby biceps and said, "Lookit me muscles, God." Mecky was nearly three when she originated her own vocabulary. She ate with her "spoony" and "forky." She put on her "socky" and "shoesy." "Me-i (her pet name), who do you love best?" "Goddy!"

I was afraid that if God was not real to them they would be unable to love him. Too many people think God is a stern, disapproving, wet blanket. For too long, we have presented religion to children as a set of rules, rituals, and dogmas and equate these with God.

I wanted my children to have an earnest belief in a real, personal God, a live, vibrant, loving reality "in whom we live and move and have our being." I wanted to share with them the God I knew. Their journeys flow from their parents' journey because that is where it begins. Faith, I have heard, is caught not taught.

How can we teach them to pray?

Kids take to prayer like fish take to water. In 1964, we began family prayer. At first, we made up a family prayer that the children repeated after us. Later, they said their own "heart prayers." After they learned to play the guitar, we sang our prayers. Phil, one of our extra children, would come with his date for "singing prayer" before they went out. After the teenagers started working, they couldn't always be present for family prayer so I would occasionally go to their rooms and pray with them.

When they wanted anything, I'd say, "Pray for it." In 1964 the World's Fair was in New York. Chrissy wanted very much to go to see the historical pavilions. I explained that we didn't have the money to pay for the tickets and the lodging in New York. "Pray for it," I told her. So she did. That week a friend from my college days called to say he was in town. I hadn't seen him in eleven years. We invited him to dinner. As he sat down at the table, he said, "I want to invite all of you to the Fair as my guests. I work at the Fair and can give you free tickets for every day you want to go. You can use my apartment while you're in New York." We haven't seen him since that visit. He was an angel.

One summer, the neighborhood children were riding their bicycles. Jack said, "Couldn't we buy bikes so we could ride around, too?" We explained to him that we couldn't afford to buy six bikes. "But pray for it." Unbelievably, three scouting families moved that summer and left us six bikes and a tricycle for Joe, the baby at the time.

When we went downtown, Rob—even as a baby—would pray for parking spaces. And we'd find them. We've prayed for money, jobs, health, inspiration, friends, bug extermination, love letters. We put up a prayer board where we could write our intentions and pray for one another. Soon, friends and neighbors came to post their intentions. Even a friend in New Jersey asked us to include his intention on the prayer board. Papa said the prayer board simplified his praying. When he got up in the morning, he would say, "Lord, board."

Why, then, isn't religion popular with kids?

For many people, God is like the President of the United States. They know he is there and that he's powerful. They also know that if they need him, he might help. But they don't call him on the phone, visit him, or have a cup of coffee with him. Neither would they exchange friendly letters. We've tried over the years to live in a way that the Father, Jesus, and the Holy Spirit are in our daily routine. It is my hope and prayer that this continues for the rest of our children's lives. I don't want God to be just the Chief Executive for them.

Do our children love God? I think so. They have all been spiritual people in varying degrees at different times in their lives. At one end of the spectrum we find the charismatic, the devout, the traditional, the conservative, and the faithful. On the other end are the questioning, the blithe, and the intermittent. In the middle we have the ecumenical, the liberal, and the Gospel Christian. In the beginning I fretted when I thought they were walking away from the Lord. But I have learned to trust two things: God loves them more than I do and if I want them saved, he wants them saved even more. Secondly, my children are as generous as I. If I respond to him, they will too—in his time and theirs. In the meantime, I pray and trust.

How do we measure our children's faith?

If indeed we must measure our children's faith, then we must look at the Lord's way of measuring. He said, "Whatever you do unto the least of these, my brethren, you do unto me." That's his measure. Or as I often quote, "You love God as much as the person you love the least."

In 1965, we made a family retreat at the Cana Colony in Aquia, Virginia, directed by the Madonna House Apostolate. Since then, we have tried to live according to the spirit of this beautiful Christian community that Catherine de Hueck Doherty founded. Basically, it is the spirit of Nazareth—hidden, little, simple. One of Madonna House's basic philosophies is "Love serves." At the time Papa became a deacon, he also became an associate of Madonna House. Diakonia is service. Love calls us out of the haven and coziness of our homes and asks us to be aware of the suffering, pain, and problems of the world outside our homes. It calls us to be a part of the solution. My prayer is that we might become branches on the Lord's vine, he living in us and we in him, so that we bear fruit abundantly. Apart from him we can do nothing.

Another charisma of Madonna House is hospitality—the national trait of Filipinos. Just as night follows day, it was apparent that we would keep an open home, allowing us to serve others within the context of our busy, demanding lives. That means simply to welcome whomever, whenever, however we can in the name of the Lord.

The gift of faith, then, is woven out of a consciousness of the presence of God: loving him, responding to him, walking beside him, serving him in each other and all others, welcoming him in them wherever we go. It begins with a desire to believe, and that invites grace. Grace increases faith; faith increases grace. The love cycle with God begins!

To start the cycle we have to understand:

- God is always there for us like a safety net, filling the holes of our inadequacies with the Spirit.
- Let Mary cover for us.
- Let God be the Lord of our lives.
- Pray for ourselves as parents. Pray especially for our children. Pray *with* our children.
- Convince our children through the personal experience of our love that God loves them. Faith is caught, not taught.
- Love serves.

Thank you, Marge Geist, Father Bernard, Father Bob, Mary Reed Newland, Teams of Our Lady, and Madonna House!

Thank you, Father, Jesus, Holy Spirit, Blessed Mother!

CHAPTER VI

CREATIVE MOTIVATION

In the beginning, I ran my ship with sheer force of will; it was efficient. But as the children grew older and the hubbub waned, I realized that this was stupid behavior. With the passing of years, my way of being a parent evolved and my parenting also changed. As I said to Bim, "Just because I may have been a dumb mother to you doesn't mean I have to continue being a dumb mother to Chip and Rob." Chip and Rob are the two youngest.

When Nini was little, she was terrified of dogs. I marched her over to Toni's Irish setter, Nikki, and barked, "Touch her! She won't hurt you. I won't let her hurt you. I just want you to see you needn't be afraid." Nini didn't budge an inch. The glare came on, the voice went up. "Either you touch her or you deal with me!" The child looked at the dog; she looked at me, then made her choice. She touched the dog.

There are many ways to skin a cat, I thought. I have vivid memories of childhood power struggles between my father and my brother, my grandmother and my sister, my uncle and my cousin: the irresistible forces and the immovable objects. I found that being an irresistible force was the natural way for me. But my heart and my mind told me that pitting will against will was a cop-out. There had to be more creative ways of being and, by golly, I was going to find them.

Ten years later, Mary was the baby. She, too, had the same fear of dogs. By then, though, I handled situations differently. This time, on gift-giving occasions, we gave Mary stuffed dogs and dog figurines, books about dogs, and dog posters. Mary became the child who took dogs—the live ones—to bed with her. Six of our children each have a dog but Nini and Mary have two each.

Logic

I gradually learned that plain, simple logic often worked. A child cried because he couldn't find a book he needed for school.

"Honey, if you cry, will you find the book?"

"No."

"Well, since that doesn't work, we better try something else." And the crying stopped. This also works with grandchildren.

Logic is effective. It surprises me that it isn't used more often. I recall an incident when I was on playground duty at school. A little girl came running to me crying, "Billy is chasing me!"

"You don't want him to chase you?"

"No."

"Then don't run. If you don't run, he can't chase you." They were both nonplussed, but it worked.

Sublimation

Then there is sublimation. Every year all thirteen of us took three weeks for wonderful camping trips to the Adirondacks, New England, Canada. Sometimes a friend or two went along. Naturally, a lot of horsing around ended in hassles. A noisy babble could hardly be called soothing when the trip would take all day. Early in the day, I would yell, "If you insist on being noisy, sing!" So we sang and sang—and sang! I taught them all the songs my father taught me and every other song I knew. Papa taught them his songs and the children taught us their songs. We sang rounds and harmonized. Shortly after we saw *The Sound of Music*, we arrived at a campsite at the day's end. Three-year-old Annie burst out of the van, ran up a hill, twirled around like Julie Andrews, and sang at the top of her little lungs, "The hills are alive with the sound of music!"

As the children grew, they went on to sing at school performances, talent shows, coffee houses, in bands and combos, at church weddings and in folk groups. Wonder of wonders, it all began because they were noisy. Another even better example of sublimation happened on a field trip with Mary's fifth grade class. At my request, I was put in charge of the boys. We sat at the back of the bus and before long they were giving the finger to the motorists behind the bus. When they realized I had seen what they were doing, they braced themselves for a severe reprimand. Instead, I said, "Do you know what the sign is for father? How about for boy? for mother? God? Jesus? Holy Spirit? friend?" They spent the rest of the trip learning sign language.

A happy and effective dynamic when working with children is to throw them off balance. When they brace themselves for a scolding, don't scold. When they think they have pushed you to tears, laugh. Whatever the reaction they expect from you, give them something else. It keeps them puzzled, intrigued, interested, and on their toes.

Play

A game usually works. In school, I don't say, "Today we'll review for the exam." Instead, I say, "Let's play Trivia! Get into two teams. Mary, you be the scorekeeper." It is such fun! Creativity says to the child, "I am not against you. I just don't want you to continue doing this silly or obnoxious thing. Let's try something that is fun for both of us." Often, children resist because it is their way of not letting you absorb them. When a power struggle begins, it bodes ill for the relationship. It becomes a you-against-me affair. But if we take the tack of "How about doing this? It might work better and could be more fun. Let's see how it will work this way." Very often the child will go along with the idea. If children don't see you as an adversary, there is nothing to fight, resist, or defend.

When Tom and Joe were in their mid-teens, we had such battles. I remarked to Pete Pallard that I couldn't understand why we had such wing-dingers when Mary Kilner and her boys didn't. I'll never forget Pete's response. "You are such a formidable woman that your sons need to knock you down figuratively in order to survive." Who, me? I always thought I was a cranky klutz but never a "formidable woman." Thank God for Pete. I took what he said to heart. I think I have succeeded in "deformidablizing" myself because Chip and Rob have not had to "knock me down."

Strengths of willpower, force, and control are useless if they engender conflict, resistance, rebellion, and all the attendant ill feelings. Imagination, creativity, and psychology may require more thinking and be more challenging but the payoff in harmony and mutual enjoyment is worth the effort. We expend energy either way. Will it be destructive or creative? We choose.

Thank you Nini, Mary, "Sounders of Music!"
Thank you, Pete Pallard!

CHAPTER VII

SHIELDING VS. EQUIPPING

Aunt May, a woman respected in our community, had raised a fine son who was her pride and joy. I listened to her reminisce about his childhood. "I didn't want him ever to be hurt. I wanted to protect him from life's troubles, take him to some mountain where nothing could hurt him and keep him safe all of his life." I was astounded at what she said. It had a major bearing on my philosophy of mothering.

Above all, it is futile to attempt to protect our children from pain. To live is to be hurt. To try to live without getting hurt is like trying to take a shower without getting wet. To deaden the hurt is to anesthetize all feelings, the good and the bad. If I had to choose between children alive enough to be hurt and children anesthetized to life, I would take the first. Living fully is such a value that I would never try to protect anyone from full life. Besides, how could I possibly trail even one child of mine, let alone eleven of them, and deflect all suffering from them?

When I expressed this to a friend, he said, "You are an unnatural mother if you don't want to protect your child from pain." I returned to the drawing board and deduced this: I want, not to protect my children from suffering, but rather to equip them with all they need to deal with pain and hurt, to meet life lovingly and see it through with gallantry and joy!

What, then, is that equipment? I start with faith in an infinitely loving God who loves us more than we can know and holds us in the hollow of his hand. Then follows unfailing love for another, love for others, compassion, humility, balance, self-acceptance. Courage, freedom, love of life, desire to learn and grow. Enthusiasm, sense of humor, health, wisdom, hope, and an affinity for joy. Then serenity and resourcefulness.

Sense of humor

Quite by accident, we discovered one of the best of these: sense of humor—Jack's gift to us. When he was in second grade, he came home complaining, "I don't like it when people keep asking me why I'm so dark. Why do they do that?"

"Because you are dark," I said.

"But I don't like it."

"Well," I suggested, "the next time someone asks you that, tell them your mother left you in the oven too long." He thought that was so funny he could hardly wait to use the quip.

Next thing we knew he was topping that answer with his own. The older kids in school enjoyed picking on the little guys. Once, when he was emptying the classroom wastebasket, one of them grabbed him by the front of his shirt menacingly. "My," Jack said in a cartoon voice, "what big beady eyes you've got!" This broke the big kid up.

His curly hair and olive skin often caused kids to call him "Nigger." To this, he would say, "Pardon me, the word is Negro." Another time, some kid on the playground asked him why he was so ugly. Placidly his comeback was "Because God didn't make me handsome like you."

Jack was born with the facility for snappy, defusing retorts that eased him out of sticky situations. Tom and Joe were not. Tom had a short fuse and Joe would feel hurt. With this variety, we invented a game we played at the dinner table. Going around the table, we would insult them. They, in turn, had to have a comeback that would make us laugh. We didn't laugh just to make them feel better either; their answers had to be genuinely funny.

I was one who was easily hurt. Sometimes I felt I had no skin or was a mollusk without a shell. Over the years, I had to find ways of living fully without being destroyed. I seem to spend a great deal of time and energy trying to discover how to live life with maximum joy.

Dealing with insults and putdowns

Eleanor Roosevelt said that no one can insult us without our permission. Chrissy has not given anyone that permission since she was five. She had come running to me where I was weeding a flower bed. "Mommy," she lamented, "Alan says I'm fat."

"Are you fat?"

"Yes."

"Then there's nothing to get upset about. It's like being told you have two feet and black hair. It's a fact." She thought about that for a moment, decided it was true, and went back to play.

Soon she returned saying, "Alan says I'm a fink!"

"Are you a fink?"

"No."

Without even looking at her, I kept right on weeding and said, "Look at the sky, Chrissy. The sky is red. Tell me; did it turn red?"

"No."

"Well, don't you see that Alan's calling you a fink doesn't make you one anymore than my saying the sky is red makes it red." She debated that for a moment and then went off to play for the rest of the afternoon without further mishap.

Only I can diminish myself. Chip discovered this when he was in the fourth grade. He came home one day quite dejected because a classmate had put him down.

"Tell me, Chip, are you less good now than you were this morning?"

"No."

"Less loved?"

"No."

"Less smart?"

"No."

"Less handsome?"

"No."

"Less anything?"

"No."

"You see? Nothing has happened to you. You are not less anything now than you were before your classmate made that remark. But he is—he is less kind."

People are for loving

Menachim Begin said at a Camp David meeting, "The task of all life is to make of every enemy a friend and of every stranger a neighbor." People who are hard to love need loving the most.

I was on the phone when Ben, five, came rushing to me, screaming, "Lisa hit me!" Lisa is his sister, a year-and-a-half younger than he. They are Joe and Theresa's children.

"What did I tell you to do when people are mean to you?"

"Hit them back!"

"That's not what I told you. I told you to be nice to them. When Lisa hits you, kiss her back."

"Kiss her!" he sputtered.

"Yes, Ben, go kiss her."

He hesitated, then walked over to Lisa. By this time, she had her arms outstretched. They hugged each other.

Edwin Markham cannot be improved upon:

> He drew a circle that shut me out,
> Heretic, rebel, a thing to flout;
> But Love and I had the wit to win:
> We drew a circle that took him in.

Compensating

If you have a handicap, you learn to compensate. If your child has a trait that gets him into trouble, do you teach him how to compensate? If we learn to compensate and teach our children to do the same, we have fantastic equipment for life. Because I have numerous handicaps, I have had to compensate frequently.

My favorite way to compensate is to pretend I am someone who has the virtue I lack. I wanted to be gentle so I pretended to be Mary Kilner. When I got up in the morning, I'd say, "Today I'm Mary Kilner" and then assume her persona. Coming downstairs, I'd see the kids throwing toast at one another, fighting, or goofing off. Had I come down as myself, I would have banged their heads together. But coming down as Mary Kilner, I said softly, "Now angels, let's get on with breakfast." For serenity, I was Mary Ann Babendreier. To curb my loquaciousness, I was Mary Ann Super.

Playing the comeback game with Tom and Joe taught them how to compensate. Helping a child determine why he is often angry is another way. After I discovered that a food allergy triggered my bad temper, I often considered food allergies as a possible cause for a child's recurring bad moods. If a child tended to be critical, I asked him to find a virtue to compensate for every fault he found in a particular individual. Emily was shy so she and Jack rehearsed on how to act when they met new people. When a child was tactless, I posed this question: "How would you feel if someone said the same thing to you?" The possibilities are endless.

Perspective can change numerous views. John Powell, S.J., author of *Why Am I Afraid To Love?* points this out. If we help our children look at things with humor, objectivity, and a sense of their own worth, it is better than shielding them. We allow them to meet life with open arms and embrace it. But first and foremost, we must learn this lesson ourselves.

Thank you, Jack and Tom, Joe and Chrissy, and Chip!
Thank you, Ben and Lisa!

CHAPTER VIII

THE CRUCIAL FACTOR

Over the years, I read every available book and article I could find that would help me become a better parent. I'd sort the information in my head and heart—chaff and grain together—then keep what was worth keeping and discard the rest. I filed some but tucked most of it into my memory file.

One article stated that no matter the damage a mother might inflict on her children, an effective father could undo it. Recently, I heard that children learn most of what they know from their mothers but get their faith from their fathers. That is indicative of the power of fathers. Although many fathers are absentee fathers, happily there is a growing trend today where young fathers participate to a great extent in the care of their children. Praise God!

Papa was one of these participating fathers long before it was a trend. His favorite way to help was to take over all the children when he got home. The kids recall, "My favorite memory was to sit on the floor around Papa as we watched TV after he got home. As soon as we heard the car come up the driveway, we raced to see who could get to Papa first—Mama did!"

To the little ones—translated "before teens"—he was the gentle parent, the one they went to when they were hurt or had nightmares. One night, Mecky came to our room and whispered, "Papa ..." I sat bolt upright and demanded, "What do you want?" She said softly and respectfully, "I'm talking to Papa, Mom." She had had a nightmare and she knew her father would give her the compassion she needed.

In some families, the oft-heard threat is, "Just wait till your father gets home!" Well, I couldn't do that. That's like serving dinner after the stew got cold and the jello melted. Fighting the battles was my responsibility. After the war was over and we signed the peace treaty, the child went to Papa to tell him what had transpired. I always had the feeling that they'd rather tangle with me a hundred times than to "fess up" to Papa even when all he would usually say was, "Oh, I'm so disappointed."

Do I give the impression that Papa is a pussycat? Papa is a bear—sometimes teddy, sometimes grizzly. If I brook no nonsense, Papa brooks even less. To the big ones—the teenagers—he held the line, the limits-setter. Kids need one tough parent and one gentle one. Certainly ours did. Papa and I simply switched roles when the children became adolescents.

On one occasion, Joe and I had a wing-ding of a fight. Looking at his angry face, I thought "My gosh, this kid is so big that if he takes me on, I'm a goner!" Almost in response to this thought, I spat out at him, "Listen! Physically you may be bigger than I but psychically I'm bigger than you!" The battle raged and waned. By the time Papa got home, Joe and I had kissed and made up. As Papa came up the steps, Joe turned to the other kids and said, "Hey, guys, here comes Mama's psychic strength!"

Usually, when I was having a disagreement with any of the kids or they were having disagreements among themselves, Papa stayed out of the picture. It was his way of saying he believed we could handle the situation ourselves. But no one doubted what would happen if anyone went too far. We all knew he was our psychic strength.

If he didn't like the way I was handling a situation, he would simply say, "That's enough." Then the dialogue between the two of us began behind the scenes where we worked out a solution satisfactory to both of us. This was of prime importance since it made clear to the kids that they could not pit us against each other.

Papa is the "old country" Papa. And why not? He is from the old country. He is deferred to, doted on, and taken care of. His word is final. Papa is also big in both senses of the word. When he realizes he is wrong, he is quick to apologize and is forgiving. He is lavish with his affection and our children never doubt he cherishes them.

"Mom, what's wrong with Papa? He's been such a grouch!"

"He's under a lot of pressure at work and he's very tense."

Ann says, "Okay, you guys, let's make him feel better and make a big fuss over him." She fixes his favorite dinner. Joe gets ice cream. Mary cleans his room. Chip makes tea and Rob does a quick job of making the house look extra nice. When they hear the car coming, they race to meet him just the way they did when they were little. But Joe was now nineteen, Ann, seventeen, Mary, fifteen, Chip, thirteen, and Rob, twelve. That's the kind of relationship they have with Papa.

Many of the children are grown and have families of their own now; Papa is retired. But he chops wood for the boys and plows the girls' gardens. He takes joy in baby-sitting and when the babies visit us, he lies down with them for their naps just as I did with their parents. When the kids were young, he took us camping and taught us the outdoor skills that went with the adventure. We became so adept that we could pitch camp and break camp in forty-five minutes—and we had four tents! He gardens with the grandchildren and takes them fishing and camping. He delights in doing things with the entire family.

Vacation time was always our best time because we could all be together. It was one nonstop party. To an only child like Papa, the merry tumult was a dream come true! In 1986, before Rob, our youngest, entered the Naval Academy at Annapolis, Papa engineered an entire clan trek to Combermere, Canada. We were all there—all forty-one of us!

I believe children need to know from their father that they are important—very important—to him. They need to know they are essential, not incidental in his life, that they are central in his scheme of things, not interruptions. They need to know that he cherishes them and is proud of them and will come to their aid when they need it. They need to hear him say he loves them. Fathers may not realize it but children often put the face of God on their father. Their image of God is a reflection of their father.

I don't believe it is written anywhere that nurturing is restricted to the mother. Children need nurturing from both parents. Often the role assigned to the father is that of executive (supreme power), legislative (maker of laws), judiciary (interpreter of laws), police (enforcer of the law). But a family is not a nation, and in the family the dynamic should be, as Jesus said, that love is the law (Mt. 22:34-40).

What does being father mean? Father is giver and maintainer of life. He is source of love and strength, inviter to fullness of growth, protector from harm, teacher, primer of wisdom, fun-starter, celebrant, healer of hurts, guide to the Kingdom, role model, fellow-pilgrim, childhood friend, unfailing support, inspiration. A father forgives sins, listens into being, mirrors God, transmits values, dispels fear, is refuge in danger, comforts, trusts. Above all, he is a fallible human being who tries to love as best he can.

This is what a father is meant to be. But fathers may not meet these expectations because no one has ever really defined fatherhood.

Replace the word mother for father. Parenthood is the same for both; that is, bringing forth, sustaining, and building life. It is not a you-go-your-way-I-go-my-way proposition. We need each other to be the best parents we can be. When one of us does not understand the children, the other has to translate for us. When we are unable to see what is happening, we have to be each other's glasses. When we do not hear what is being said, we have to be each other's hearing aid.

Parenthood is not a rivalry nor a competition. Parents are meant to challenge lovingly and to uphold each other in their mutual task of raising children who will be whole, loving, and free men and women. Often, however, parents are unwitting pawns in the hands of their children who pit them against each other, playing both ends against the middle and coming out on top. How often have you seen children expertly push their obliging parents' buttons, set them at each other's throats so that they can go off to do their own thing while their parents are locked in mortal combat?

When we realized how easy it was to fall into this trap, when our buttons got pushed, we closed ranks instead of turning against each other. Once it is understood that Mom and Dad cannot be triangled, the attempts to get them to take sides will dwindle.

Parents may have differing values and theories about raising children. If they come from different cultures, this is even more evident. What is totally acceptable in one culture can be taboo in another. The danger lies in one or both assuming the attitude, "There is only one right way. If you don't agree with me, then you're wrong." This calls for a lot of willing dialogue and listening. Both sides can gain so much when they look lovingly at the values of the other in a sincere desire and effort to understand. This calls for maturity. We are so quick to assume we have all the answers and stubbornly stick to one's guns even when we are proved wrong.

In some families, both sides try to convince the other of the validity of their stand as if they must agree on every issue. With us, our kids know our values and what is important to each of us and why. Papa enjoys hunting and I don't; that's fine. I enjoy art museums and

Papa doesn't; that's fine. I don't have to go hunting and Papa doesn't have to go to art museums. Our kids enjoy both.

When we face an important issue that we cannot resolve, we agree to consult a third party who is an authority on the matter, using the premise that we will abide by whatever this authority counsels. Amazingly, this is a quick and simple solution. But this is possible only when neither of us is out to prove who holds the power in the family. As the saying goes, "Where there is love, there is no will to power."

The crucial factor in happy parenting is the other parent.

Thank you, Papa!

CHAPTER IX

SINGLE PARENTING

As I was writing these chapters, I gave them to the children to critique. Chip did a lot of it because he was always around when I was writing. After reading the last chapter he asked, "What if you're a single parent?" Good question.

Over the years I've observed that no matter how much pain exists between a man and a woman, if it doesn't spill over onto their children, the children can weather the rough spots fairly well. If single parents can gift their children with the image of their other parent as okay and loving them, then they are co-parenting still.

But what if the other parent is a jerk? Let the children find that out for themselves *without your help*, just as the other parent should let them find out who you really are without his/her help. In other words, parents—whether married, divorced or never married—should not pollute with their own bitterness their children's relationship with the other parent.

The temptation is to use the children as weapons and artillery against each other. In this case, however, the weapons/artillery are human beings and they, too, are destroyed in one's attempt to retaliate against the other.

I am acquainted with two such families. In the first family, the father was a flagrant adulterer. The children, nevertheless, turned out well and two of them are missionaries. In the second family, there was no adultery but several of the children have dysfunctional lives. This puzzled me and I mentioned it to Papa. He pointed out that in the first family, the mother never belittled her husband despite his adulterous behavior. In the second, the mother took every opportunity to put her husband down even when he was a hardworking, faithful husband. So I reiterate: To treat the child's other parent without rancor is to gift the child.

Perhaps a built-in hazard in single parenting is guilt. Many single parents seem to operate with an undercurrent of guilt and this guilt tends to make them vulnerable to their children's manipulation. At best, all parents are susceptible to this, but the single parent is singularly so.

What about the family where one parent dies? In such a circumstance, children often find a parent image. My mother died when I was a very young child, and I looked for mothering from anyone who would give it. Though my grandmother, Nanay, was my main mother figure, I had two loving aunts, Mang and Manang, who did much of the mothering. I also gravitated to an uncle's wife for her gentleness, to another because of the things she taught me, and to a third because she took an interest in me. I did not live with my father so I was drawn to this uncle who lovingly surfaced and cultivated my gifts.

All I have said thus far about fun parenting holds true for single parents. The difficulties arise when one parent assumes the role of mother and father and has no one to share the pressures of day-to-day living. Dual parenting demands maturity, but single parenting demands heroic maturity.

Thank you, Chip!
Thank you, Mang and Manang!

* * *

Reprise

These, then, are the basics of fun parenting:

- The primary function of parents is to help their children discover how wonderful they are.
- Love without discipline is not love. Discipline without love is not discipline.
- Intimidate them. It's efficient.
- Saturate your children in a solution of love the first three years of their lives and they will feel loved for as long as they live.
- God loves us and is our safety net.

- Avoid the power struggle. Try the creative approach: sublimation, psychology, logic.
- Protecting your children from suffering is a futile exercise. Try, rather, to equip them with all they need to meet life lovingly and to see it through with gallantry and joy!
- Parent together. The other parent is the crucial factor.
- If you are a single parent, treat your child's other parent without rancor. This is to gift the child.

"Great!" you say. "But what are these neat theories and fancy ideas like in real life?" Believe me, I learned and extracted these from real life. I am no sociologist, psychologist, philosopher, scientist, or theologian. I am an everyday type of mother who comes apart, screams, smacks, weeps, and gnashes her teeth. I even run away from home. I am called to the school office and my kids do dumb things. I do not have the answers on how to raise perfect children. I only know how to enjoy them!

THE SHORTCUTS

CHAPTER X

SETTING PRIORITIES

Let us begin with setting priorities. That is a good beginning.

My friend, Beth, has a nonstop battle with her children about the state of their bedrooms. These battles bracket their days—the first thing in the morning and the last at night.

"Wouldn't it be better if you didn't make clean rooms an issue and enjoy some harmony instead?" I suggested.

"No," she answered. "They have to learn responsibility."

I pointed out that children's bedrooms are the only places in the universe they can call their own, and we should allow them breathing places there. Periodically—for the sake of sanitation and hygiene—they should clean it up. Usually, they will if the requests are reasonably spaced, perhaps once a week or once a month depending on the child's bent for neatness and order or the absence thereof.

The children learn responsibility if we ask them to be considerate of other people and observe community rules in the rooms they share with the family. They also learn responsibility by helping with the chores around the house. Meanwhile, parents can build relationships, not tear them down, in the time they spend fighting about clean bedrooms.

What is more important to you? clean bedrooms or amicable relationships? peace at all costs or loving honesty? a well-run household or listened-to family members? going to work to have a higher standard of living or staying at home for more time with the family? We sometimes must choose between one or the other. If you can have your cake and eat it too, more power to you.

We had been married almost nine years, and I was struggling desperately to have well-cared-for, happy children with a decently run house and a cheerful disposition. I was a total wreck—a failure. The six kids—the oldest was six—wore socks that didn't match and sported all the telltale signs of having a mother who wasn't on the ball. Our basement was a living organism I fondly referred to as the Black Hole of Calcutta. I was a screaming meemie who made real an epithet a Jesuit priest gave me in my teen years. He called me the wrath of God.

One evening, enroute home from a visit with Leo and Toni Fisher, I said to Papa, "I have come to the conclusion that I am unable to deliver the three things I want to give you: good and happy children, a well-run household, and a cheerful wife to come home to. I can deliver only two. Pick whatever combination you want." Without hesitation he said, "I want good and happy children and a cheerful wife." He set my priorities and from that time on I worked on those.

As much as I'd like to have a beautiful, clean, orderly house, I am unable to accomplish that goal. There is always a child who needs attention at the same time the house does. In the desire to have an ideal environment, I might subconsciously consider a messy child a terrible nuisance, an interruption in my carefully planned day, a schedule bumper. My vibes, I'm afraid, would say this to my child and he'd surely pick them up. I don't want this to ever happen.

A familiar plaque says, "My house is clean enough to be healthy and dirty enough to be happy." That says it all for me. I don't want a house so lovely that everyone has to make sure it stays that way. I want my house to be a home that people can enjoy and be comfortable in.

Lillian Gilbreth, mother of the *Cheaper By the Dozen* family, expressed my feelings: "Keeping a spotless house is like putting pearls on a string with no knot at the end."

After these many years, my priority is to have a house where people enjoy themselves and feel welcome and free to relax. Fun is high on my list of priorities. I went to the same school from first grade through college—Assumption Convent. The French congregation of nuns, the Religieuses de l'Assomption, taught there. Notre Mère, the mother superior, had a great influence on me. One of her most frequent sayings was, "My Dear, life is short; enjoy it!" That made a lifelong impression on me.

Often on summer evenings when the children were little, someone at the dinner table would say, "Let's go to a movie!" Another would second that idea and, as one, we'd leave the table and go to the car.

We didn't put anything away; that could wait until we returned.

Although I may appear to fight at the slightest provocation, I really do not care to fight over little things. I do fight for great causes like love and caring, kindness toward others, respect, obedience, honesty. The rest I can let go. Mary Reed Newland told us, "If you fight them on the little things, you lose them on the big ones." They dismiss you as a quarrelsome martinet; thus, when you raise a valid issue, no one listens. But when you choose the issues you defend, it is likely that they will pay attention.

Phil, our "singing prayer" fan, and his wife, Tonia, had a discussion about nagging. I said I didn't nag much, but Phil begged to differ; he often called me the nag of his life. I stood my ground. I didn't nag about clothes, brushing teeth, schoolwork, grades, or the state of their bedrooms. I did, though, expect the children to be good and kind to each other and respectful of others, especially their elders; to assume their share of responsibilities around the house; to be prayerful, obedient, honest, sensitive, open, giving, and caring.

There may be times when our own priorities differ from the way others see them. This may be due to self-deception, mixed signals, or misinterpretation. For an interesting exercise, invite family members to consider what they perceive to be the priorities of the others. Start with the question, "What do you think is the most important thing in the world to me?" That can be an eye opener for a lively discussion at the dinner table. Try it!

Thank you, Notre Mère!

CHAPTER XI

BASIC SHORTCUTS

Parents may succeed in making parenting more fun; however, it's never easy—easier, perhaps, but not easy. A few basic principles will facilitate matters considerably.

1. Be consistent. If you don't want your children to eat between meals, then don't ever let them eat between meals. If you forbid them on Monday and allow them on Tuesday because you're too tired to argue with them, then it becomes a game called Mama Roulette: "Let's see if we can get Mom to give us a between-meal snack today." They perceive it as a matter of moods—your moods. If they understand that no matter what your mood, you will not allow them to eat between meals, then they won't bother to ask anymore. Most people have trouble being consistent. I don't. I'm consistently mean.

2. Carry out your threats: Have you ever heard parents say, "Stop that or I'll send you to your room"? The child doesn't stop. Then begins the vicious circle: the threat, the nonconformance until the day's end. Such action is meaningless and you lose your credibility. The action that is effective says, "Stop that or I'll send you to your room." Unacceptable behavior continues. "All right. You may go to your room now." Enforce. End of story.

3. Don't make inane threats such as "Do as I tell you or I'll break your neck." I, on occasion, made threats that made me feel ridiculous when I carried them out. Nini always dawdled in the morning. Getting her ready for school was an absolute ordeal. I told her, "If you don't finish your oatmeal by the time the long hand of the clock reaches twelve, I'll clap the whole bowl on your head!" Any other child would have gobbled the oatmeal and left. Not Nini. A spoonful was left when the long hand reached twelve. Looking me straight in the eye, she deliberately put half a spoonful into her mouth. Subsequently, I clapped the bowl onto her head, necessitating a shampoo on top of everything else. That was a learning experience for Mama.

4. *Don't allow the child to ignore an instruction.* This applies especially to toddlers. If they understand this, it will not be a problem when they get older. The first instruction you cannot let them ignore is "Come here." When they don't mind, simply go to them and say in a firm tone of voice, "When I call, you come," then take them where you want them. It may take time and effort, but it saves hassles later. It is a down payment on future obedience.

When you let a child do as he pleases because it's too much trouble to fight him, you are simply postponing fights for when he gets older and harder to manage. If you invest the time and trouble when the child is little, you simplify your own life and that of the child because habit makes cooperation automatic. In earlier years, one of my frequent sayings was, "If I can't get you to____now when you are knee-high, I might as well turn in my mother's badge because I won't be able to do it when you tower over me and drive your own car." Many people, nonetheless, prefer to postpone than to invest early. That is an enigma to me.

5. *Never make it profitable for a child to behave badly.* If a child gets what she wants when she throws fits, it's reasonable to believe that she will keep throwing them—it's profitable. If a child wears you down by hassling you, she will persist in hassling until she gets her way. If you give in to whims when she fusses, she will use that ploy until you acquiesce. When a child of mine threw a fit, I would throw one, too. His reaction was, "Never mind...." At other times I would begin with, "You don't know what a hard time is until I give it to you...." Often, the exchange stopped there. I was the proverbial sleeping dog they were happy to let lie.

At this point you may be thinking, "How can you enjoy parenthood with all that hassling?" The truth is, hassling is synonymous with the way football is to a football player. It takes as much energy and effort as construction work, but football is a game. The work is part of the game and, consequently, it is fun. To me, hassling is a battle of wits, and if I can outwit my little hassler, then it's not bad at all.

Joe was fussing about having to wash dishes on his day. "Fuss about the day," I said, "and I'll give you the week. Fuss about the week, and you get the month. Fuss about the month and you'll wash dishes every day of the year." Snarl. Glare. Cheerful dishwasher, that

Joe. Then there are kids who try to call your bluff. Mary was one such. Who do you think fixed breakfast every day for a whole year?

6. *Eye contact is vital.* When you have a discussion with your little friend, make sure you look into each other's eyes. Some people believe they have no commitment to anything if there is no eye contact. When you look directly at each other, there is no way either of you can pretend the other isn't listening. Joe always tried to avoid my eyes. I simply pointed my index and middle fingers straight at his eyes quickly as if to poke them, and just as quickly snapped my hand back, pointing to mine and saying, "Look at me!" It always worked.

7. *Have them play back what you said to make sure they understand you correctly.* That exercise must come from the teacher in me, but it is important. It is amazing how they misunderstand what you say. When the children were little, I read them the Passion of Jesus on Good Friday afternoon. The last line of the story is "And the centurion said, 'Verily, this man was the Son of God.' "

My first question was "Who died on the cross?"

The five year old, innocent little face turned upward, answered, "The brother of Jesus!"

"The brother of Jesus?"

"Yes, the centurion said he was the Son of God. So he must be the brother of Jesus!"

8. *Keep your energy level and stamina high.* Eat nourishing meals. Take vitamin and mineral supplements. Rest adequately and take mini-vacations—ten minute ones in the bathroom are ideal. In our house that was the only room with a lock, and it is still my prayer room. Exercise, pray, and meditate. I recommend B-complex vitamins for stronger nerves and stamina and calcium for serenity. Vitamins formulated for stress are good. Take good care of your body. When you keep fit, you will be equal to whatever your children have to dish out.

One of my favorite showdown stoppers was "You wanna fight? You really wanna fight?" spoken eyeball to eyeball, nose to nose. Understandably, that won't be too effective if your eyeballs are bleary and you have bags under your eyes.

When Tom was about three, he said to me in a moment of great anger, "Just wait 'til I get big...."

And I said, "Listen you! I don't care if you get as big as Mr. Cole and twice as strong as Butch, I'll lick all of you put together with one hand tied behind my back!" The vehemence and energy behind that claim made it convincing. No one has ever tried to find out whether I could really do that.

For years, I believed I was a vicious-tempered person until I discovered at thirty-nine that it was a food allergy! When I ate wheat, I got sick, fierce, and depressed. If I tried to cheat, my loving children and friends would snatch the wheat goodie from my hand or mouth. Much to my joy and relief, I discovered that I could have good children without tantrums and towering rages. I may have intimidated them, but no one was terrified of me! It was never terror. It was something more than that. I call it the grace of God.

It was the Holy Spirit who led me to the basic eight shortcuts of parenting:

1. Be consistent.
2. Carry out your threats.
3. Don't make inane threats.
4. Don't allow a child to ignore instruction.
5. Never make it profitable for a child to behave badly.
6. Keep eye contact. That's vital.
7. Have them play back what you say to make sure they understand correctly.
8. Keep your energy level and stamina high.

Thank you, Holy Spirit!

CHAPTER XII

SIBLING POWER

Perhaps the greatest untapped resource for optimum fun in family life is sibling power. Like nuclear power, sibling power has the potential for good on the one hand and destruction on the other hand. Because Neng and I were sibling rivals, it was important to me that my children not mirror us.

We decided on preventive action. When we were sure that Bim was on the way, we told Chrissy about it. She was all of six months. What would a six month old understand about such things? I believe it is better to tell little ones things they probably don't understand. It would be worse not to tell them things on the supposition that they don't understand when, in fact, they do. I work on the premise that it is better to pour a quart of water into a pint jar to fill it to capacity than to pour only a cup in because, then, it will be only half full.

We told Chrissy that God and we were making a baby just for her. When the baby began to move, she would pat it, kiss it, and "talk" to it. The day we came home from the hospital, Chrissy was waiting at the door for us. We placed Bim in her arms saying, "Here's your baby, Honey." We did the same for each of the children down the line. They have had proprietary feelings toward their "babies" even as adults.

There was another system in operation. The Big Guys had special babies among the Little Guys. Chrissy was second Mom to Bim, Jack, Nini, and Meck; Bim to Tom and Joe; Jack to Ann; Nini to Mary and Chip; and Mecky to Rob. When we walked to the supermarket—I don't drive—Chrissy, eight, pushed the stroller with Tom, two; Bim, seven, held the hand of Mecky, four; Jack, six, and Nini, five, held each other's hand.

When Chrissy was in college, she took Rob to school with her. I know of no other person who went to college before kindergarten. Nini and Mecky took the Little Ones—Annie, Mary, Chip, and Rob—with them on their dates.

When it was time to nurse Ann, I'd say to Joe, who was twenty-three months, "C'mon, Joe, it's loving time for our baby and us." We'd lie in bed with Annie between us; he'd snuggle up to her. When I nursed her on the other side, I'd lie between them and he'd snuggle up to me. It was a warm, loving time for the three of us. Joe and Ann were especially close when they were growing up.

Perhaps the two closest are Chip and Rob, who are twenty months apart. They enjoy each other and are still close friends at twenty-eight and twenty-six. Some of the other children, however, called each other best friends until they were older and changed into different people. On the other hand, Jack, Tom, Joe, Chip, and Rob are closer as mature adults than they were as children. Maturity seems to have deepened their capacity for friendship.

We have a friend with five children who proudly says, "I treat each one as if he or she were an only child." Papa, an only child, says, "Why would anyone want to treat his children that way?"

Many parents tend to the needs of their children in this way; they make themselves central, always trying to meet their children's needs:

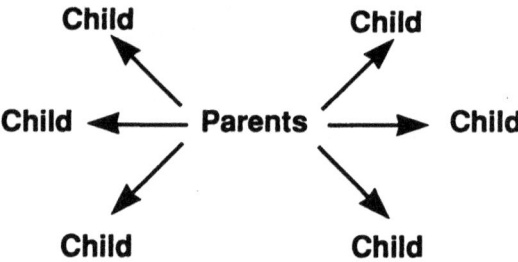

This system is exhausting and sibling power is never tapped. Often it fosters sibling rivalry.

In the sibling power system, on the other hand, all giving is mutual. Siblings tend to each other's needs; parents and children take care of each other. The multiple interaction makes an incredibly strong framework for relationships that are woven into lasting bonds. We become each other's visible guardian angels and the family's built-in rescue system. We are each other's psychotherapists and cheerleaders. It might be diagrammed in this way:

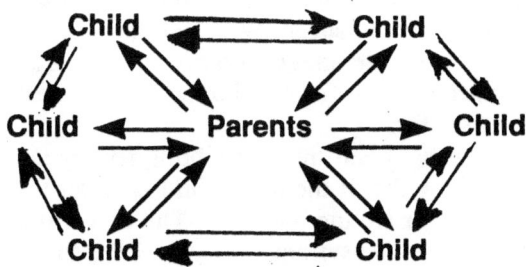

We do not believe in bailing out; nevertheless, our children have often helped each other through tight spots. They are supportive when it comes time to baby-sit, move, or do work on each other's houses. They lend each other money, share clothes, cut hair, pray for, and pamper each other.

When I take one to task, one or the other becomes his defense attorney. When Tom got into trouble as a kid, Meck would get upset if she thought we were too severe with him. How dare we be mean to her "baby"!

When the Big Girls were little, they stood in line to button the back of each other's dresses. The children delivered newspapers. On summer mornings we'd hear them coming down the street singing in harmony. They cleaned the kitchen the same way—making work light by turning it into a musical enterprise.

Perhaps the best way to unleash sibling power in the family is to first ask the question, "What causes sibling rivalry?"

One of the most common reasons is favoritism. Some people don't hide their preferences. A successful parent is the one who convinces each child that he or she is the favorite. I work on that premise. When I ask, "Who do you think is my favorite?" the boys claim it's Jack and Jack claims it's Rob. Only Chip has the right answer: "I am." I work toward that day when they all will say, "I am."

One of my little friends felt I picked on him and loved the others more than he. You see, he was always in hot water. So I explained, "If we could count good feelings, then I have ten points for each of you every morning. I come to the kitchen and see that Chrissy has breakfast going. She now has eleven points. I call all of you and two are missing. You're both down to nine. The other one comes down and says, 'Sorry I'm late. I was in the bathroom when you called.' She's back to ten. I start looking for you and find you reading the comics. You're down to eight. I'm unhappy about that and you throw a fit. You're now down to seven. Who lost the good feelings for you? Somebody else? Me?" He understood my strategy and admitted what he thought was favoritism for his siblings was, in reality, something he was responsible for.

Another factor that contributes to sibling rivalry is age difference. Recent studies show that if the older child is under two or over four, chances are better for sibling harmony. The two children we refer to later in this chapter—Teaser and Teased—were the only two of the eleven who didn't exactly amuse each other; they are thirty-two months apart. The first five are a year apart and the last five were twenty, twenty-one, and twenty-three months apart. Our experience, then, bears out that study.

A third cause is comparisons. "Why can't you be like...?" This is difficult because we often do it without much thought. Happily, my children call my hand when I do it. Report cards frequently elicit comparisons.

My sister, Neng, and I were the only two growing up together. Each of us was held up as a model for the other. "Why can't you be as hardworking (mature, responsible) as Neng?" Or vice versa, "Why can't you be as pleasant (or friendly) as Inday?" So we viewed each other as competitors and rivals. "The family often described us as "cat" and "dog." I regret those years when we did not see ourselves as friends. Thank God, maturity changed that.

I decided to use brainwashing techniques on our children. When they fought, I made them stand in front of each other, look into each other's eyes and repeat, "Brothers and sisters are for loving." If they bolted, I tied them together. (I wasn't a scoutmaster's wife for nothing.) Invariably, the charade was so silly that they would eventually burst out laughing, and that defused the situation. I wouldn't let them go, though, until they did laugh. Some were stubborn enough to hold out for a while. They were the same youngsters who would bolt. I left them tied as they walked about the house pulling against each other. They learned a bonus lesson. If they pulled against each other, the rope hurt; if they took turns doing what the other wanted, it didn't. After a time, I no longer needed to use the rope.

This worked well with the younger children but, understandably, not with teenagers. Try corralling two lads bigger than yourself and have them say to each other, "Brothers are for loving." I didn't do that. I'm not that naive.

At this time, Papa and I were taking a course on family systems therapy. We were to apply the principles we learned in class to family problems. The constant fighting between Number Two Son and Number Three Son was a concern. Father Francis Walsh, our teacher, said, "I suppose you tell the teaser to stop teasing and the teased to stop getting upset."

"Yes we do, Father."

"You have both of them believing you are siding with the other, confirming to them what they already fear—you prefer the one over the other."

"What do we do?"

"Tell the teaser he isn't teasing enough. Tell the teased he should get more upset. In fact, tell them to kill each other."

"Father! They will."

"Just try it, then tell me the outcome at our next class."

As expected, a battle was in progress when we got home. I did exactly what Father suggested. To my utter disbelief, it worked like a charm. When I said, "Do me a favor, you two. Kill each other!" they were so stunned that there was no fighting for the rest of the night. I have passed this tactic on to many beleaguered parents. Those who have braved it have seen it work like magic. When one in the system changes stance, the other is forced to change. That is what happens.

When Rob was little, I praised him for a drawing he gave me. He said, "But I don't draw as good as Chip." I answered, "But you draw as good as Rob and that's important." I like to think he took my word for it. When Chip was a senior, he won first prize in the art show and Rob got the coach's award for track. Each boy has his own strengths and gifts and each of them rejoices with the other.

Sibling power does this. It unleashes latent power in the family—power that can destroy envy, jealousy, resentment, competition, and rivalry and replace them with friendship, a lifetime of strong affection and support, and nonstop good times together.

Sibling power is set in motion when—

1. children feel they belong to each other, not dethroned by the other,
2. children look after and support each other and their parents,
3. parents show no favoritism in the family,

4. the older baby is either too young to know better or mature enough to make room for a new member in the family,
5. parents make no comparisons among the children,
6. children are made to see that their brothers and sisters are for loving, and
7. each child knows what his or her own gifts and strengths are.

Thank you, Chris, Bim, Jack, Nini, Meck, Tom, Joe, Ann, Mary, Chip, and Rob.

CHAPTER XIII

FIGHTING THE GOOD FIGHT

Anger and fighting are not dirty words in our scheme of things. They are as much a part of life as airing bedrooms and scrubbing floors. Coming from a culture where people readily expressed their anger, I found it amazing that in American culture anger is often a no-no. Maybe the reason for this is the failure to distinguish between constructive anger and destructive anger/fighting. The first kind moves toward resolutions; the second doesn't.

When Phil and Mecky were going together, he happened upon one of our "airing bedroom" scenes. Someone was being chewed out in public; it was a culture shock to Phil who is German-Irish. He said, "If things like that were said at our house—and they never are—the rest of us would look at each other in silence; it would be a major crisis and the person concerned would need to move out. What's even more shocking is that it didn't bother your other kids. They merely turned up the volume on the TV so they could hear above your voices."

Find emotional trash cans

Phyllis had so much pent-up anger that the courts suggested she undergo psychotherapy. I explained that what happened to her was comparable to the condition of a house where the occupants store their trash and garbage in the basement for thirty years—accumulated gases will blow the roof off.

Some people drive their psychic garbage—strong emotions and intense negative feelings—underground just like Phyllis had done. Others erupt every hour on the hour at the slightest provocation.

They are like people who open their windows and throw their trash and garbage out on the yard. Phyllis questioned, "What do you do with your psychic trash and garbage?"

"The same thing you do with any trash and garbage. Put it into containers and dispose of it in an orderly manner."

"What containers?"

Bim had taught me about these containers. She had a short fuse and incidents would get to her long before they got to Chris or Jack. One night I went into their room to say goodnight. I saw a sheaf of papers on the floor with monsters drawn on them. Under each monster was the name of Bim's teacher. "This is terrible!" I exclaimed.

"Mom," Chris said with all her grade-school wisdom, "her teacher doesn't know anything about it; she isn't hurt and it relieves Bim. She tapes them on the wall every night and spits on them."

That's an emotional trash can.

Different people have different trash cans. Jeannette Cole cooks. Marge Keithline scrubs floors or washes windows. Some people jog; others chop wood. I sing Peggy Lee's "Pass Me By" at the top of my lungs. Once, in a high state of exasperation just before supper time, I was singing in full force. A neighbor child playing in the basement with the boys remarked, "Boy, your mom sure is happy." The boys said casually, "Oh, no. When she sings like that, it means she's very angry." At other times I play—rather—I pound on the piano with great vehemence. Once I even bruised my fingertips!

I suggest that the kids find their own emotional containers. Tom needed a punching bag, but I never bought him one. (Now, since he's married and has two boys of his own, he bought one.) I used to make Joe run around the block.

Anger isn't bad

Anger is not bad, but it should be expressed in nondamaging ways. It need not result in a ruptured relationship. Over the years, we have developed constructive ways of fighting. Try not to accuse or blame. Make simple statements: "It really upsets me when...." "I did not mean to hurt you; I'm sorry." "Please don't see hurt where none was meant." "Are you being sarcastic?"

Loud voices are acceptable as long as the words are respectful. It's hard to control decibels when your adrenaline is running on high. When a child was insolent in my "verduga" days, he got a smack on the mouth. I have since learned to say quite calmly, "I don't deserve that disrespect. It's possible to say what you feel without hurting anyone that badly." This works well. Part of the reason is that I'm talking now to young adults.

More than once someone has asked me, "How can you expect your children to control their tempers when you have such a bad one yourself? How do you justify your rages?" Well, when I'm in the throes of a major rage, I say to them, "You had better learn to deal with your tempers now while you still can or you'll grow up to be just like me!" Then I lean over with my ugliest angry face and say in my loudest voice, "How would you like to be just like me?" When they shake their heads I know I got my point across.

Clarification of issues

Mary was my student. In distress she once said, "I hate it when we fight." "We aren't fighting, my dear," I responded. "We are clarifying issues. If we don't clarify these issues, we will not stay friends." At that time she was a sophomore in high school. Now she is in college—and we are still close friends.

It is necessary to clarify meanings to maintain healthy relationships. Amazingly, two people can attach different meanings to the same sentence. Have you seen the plaque that says, "I know you think you understand what I said, but I'm not sure you realize that what you think you heard is not what I meant."

Joe often says to me, "Assume nothing." Check what the other has understood you to say. Conversely, reiterate to the other what you think he said. Frequently there is a discrepancy.

Tom was going out for the evening. "What time will you be home, Dear?"

"Oh, early." That meant before midnight to me.

He came in at 1:30 a.m. to find a livid mother. "I thought you'd be home early. It's past midnight!"

"Mom, it isn't two yet!" Early to him meant before two.

Forgiving

When Papa and I gave talks on marriage to high school students, invariably someone would ask if we fought in front of our children. Papa's answer was, "Naturally. You can't stage spontaneous combustion. But we also apologize and forgive each other in front of them." Forgiveness is the middle name of love.

Forgiveness is difficult. I don't believe I could forgive if I were left to myself. But forgiving others is the condition Jesus put on our being forgiven. I have much I need to be forgiven for so I, in turn, had better forgive.

Reconciliation happens when someone says, "I'm sorry. Please forgive me." It happens, too, when someone forgives even when the other hasn't yet apologized. Children whose parents apologize to them will have an easier time apologizing and forgiving.

When a child hurts someone, it is better to ask, "What do you have to say for yourself?" than "Say you're sorry!" In reality, the child probably doesn't feel sorry, but with the question, you give him the opportunity to explain his position and to talk about it. If he has hurt you, it helps him if you tell him how you feel. "I felt letdown when you wouldn't help me at suppertime because I really needed your help." Although many kids might call this "laying a guilt trip," don't let that be a problem. They should feel guilty.

Brent didn't want to live with his parents any longer and he made arrangements to find another home. Ours was a possibility. He spoke bitterly about the wrongs his parents had dealt him. As we walked to the store I said, "Brent, everything your parents have done to you, we have done to our children. The only difference is that our children forgive us. I don't know why, but they always do. Praise God!"

Silence is not necessarily peace

Friends have told me their parents never fought but the tension between them was so intense that it was almost too painful to tolerate. "I often wished they had gotten a divorce." Constructive conflict is to a relationship what cleanser is to a tub. Forgiveness is the rinsing water and a well-cleaned relationship shines!

When we are able to be truthful and to fully express to each other what we feel, we can afford to be close. On the other hand, if we mask or bottle up our real feelings, we will discover eventually that we can no longer afford to continue a relationship; it costs too much. The other attendant danger in bottling one's real thoughts and feelings is that the backup becomes so heightened that it is impossible to let some of it out without breaking the dam altogether. Expressing feelings as things happen makes them bite-sized and poses little trouble. This can be as simple as "Ouch, that hurts!"

But to acquire the privilege of being honest with someone, we must first love them. We do not have a right to honesty if we don't love the other. In other words, speak your mind lovingly to create a free atmosphere in the home. In such an environment no one should go around seething with unspoken rage or having others wonder how he or she feels. It doesn't become necessary to drop hints and innuendoes to effect changes. These ploys are energy consuming and confusing. They also take away time that could be spent enjoying each other.

To fight the good fight:

1. Find emotional trash cans.
2. Understand that anger and fighting are not always bad.
3. Clarify issues and meaning of statements.
4. Apologize, forgive, reconcile.
5. Show loving honesty that heals. Silence is not necessarily peace.

Thank you, Bim!

CHAPTER XIV

OPENNESS IS FREEDOM

Loving honesty engenders trust, trust engenders openness, and openness engenders the freedom to be. In such an atmosphere, no one needs to say, "Don't tell Mom but ..." or "Be sure Papa doesn't find out," or "You know, Ann, Bim really bugs me when she does that. But don't tell her." Why the need to conceal?

When I was ten, we moved to a little town where people said nice things to your face but expressed their real feelings about you behind your back. People probably do that everywhere. But in that little town, people made sure you found out what others said about you behind your back. At that young age it was painful for me to learn that I could not trust people, and I made this decision: I would not be two-faced. It was important that I not lead anyone to believe I thought one way about the person when I really thought something else. Strangely, being this way does not alienate people. It makes them feel secure to know where they stand with you and, consequently, they trust you.

Parents have no problem telling their children what they think about them: "You are such a slob." And children today have little trouble telling their parents what they think about them: "I hate you!" This kind of communication is destructive.

You are working on your bank statement and you can't make the blessed thing balance with your checkbook. You've been at it for hours. Your five year old keeps demanding your attention for no particular reason. This child simply has a habit of doing this when you are absorbed in another task. If you tell her not to bother you, she will feel rejected. If she keeps coming back, you will have a major dislocation. What to do?

"Honey, come listen on the phone to what the weatherman is saying!" Dial the weather number and put the phone to her ear. While she listens, talk to her about something you want her to do. When she hangs up, ask her what the weatherman said and what you said. She will be disconcerted; she got neither message. Then explain to her why you are having difficulty with her demands for attention when you are absorbed with a task.

We often hesitate to tell others how we really feel because they may get hurt. But as Father Bob often said, "When you are mad at Jack, tell him. When you don't tell him, you tell him." Negative feelings expose themselves in vibes, body language, subconscious rejection, a cool manner, and other kinds of behavior. It is much better to articulate the problem.

Once I was so upset with Papa that I went for a long walk with Rob just to let off steam. Rob was fourteen. In the middle of my litany of complaints, he stopped me and said, "Have you told him all this?"

"No."

"Then tell *him*, Mom, not me." Rob had learned a lesson well. That had always been my standard response to the children when they complained to me about one or the other.

Telling each other how we really feel hones our skills at dialogue. Families need to learn what we now call "conflict management." I call it creative fighting: clarifying issues that lead to healing and resolution. If fighting leads only to more hurt and more anger, 'tain't creative.

Conflict management requires communication skills. Listening takes priority. When your children vent their feelings, do you really hear what they say or are you too busy defending your position of power as parent? Is your ego so fragile that you see your child's expression of frustration as an accusation about your ability to parent well? When you "dialogue," what is more important to you? getting your points across to your child or trying to understand the points the child wants to get across? Can you honestly say you respect your child as a person or is he an extension of yourself? Is respect something only your child should have for you, not you for him?"

Another reason people conceal information is to protect the other. When I was a child, our adults never told us about a crisis in order to shield us from the harsh realities of life. But crisis is felt in the air much like an impending storm. I always thought the monster was ninety feet tall when it was actually only ninety inches tall. I can still taste the fear that came from not knowing.

Remembering this, I let our children see the monsters. When we can size up the crisis for ourselves, I believe we are better able to deal with it. I do not believe in protecting. Strengthening? Yes. Protecting? No. A protected child does not learn to cope for himself if Mom and Dad are always there to bail him out. To bail a child out of every bad situation he gets into against your advice will only make his behavior a chronic one. It also postpones his growing up.

Conversely, children conceal their escapades from adults to avoid dealing with the consequences. When the Boy Scouts passed time at our house, they would tell us things they would never tell their parents. One day, I wondered out loud if our kids would be as open with us as the scouts were. They said, "If you can listen to them with the same cool that you listen to us, they will be."

I tried. Sometimes I succeeded—with great effort. Much depended on how they told me. Some of the kids—like Chrissy—were good at telling me what fool thing they had done without destroying my equilibrium. Chrissy always told it as a big joke. Bim was forthright about what she thought; when I talked with her, I pretended I was on a mental tightwire. There were those who told me nothing so I held my breath about them. Rob told me as soon as he walked through the door when and why he had gotten into trouble. I felt easiest about him.

Finally, feelings enter in. In the past, if you expressed your feelings, people would say, "You shouldn't feel that way." Or worse! "How dare you feel that way!" Today, we know there are no "shoulds" to feelings. To express one's feelings enables us to clarify what is going on inside us.

Happily, I grew up in a culture where feelings and the expression of them were okay. If you were happy, exult. If you were sad, weep. If you were angry, say so. If you were scared, admit it. If you loved someone, tell her. (Nice girls, though, didn't tell their young men. That was taboo.) If you disliked someone, tell him why. It seems we knew then what psychologists tell us today: Feelings are neither good nor bad. Acknowledge them without shame or embarrassment.

In families where communication is valued and encouraged, this accusation will invariably come up: "I feel you don't love me." This is fine. If the speaker didn't really feel loved, she would express it some other way. What she is actually saying is, "Do you really love me?" or "Am I lovable?"

"Why do you feel that way?"

"When I come home, you haven't saved any food for me; when I want to talk to you, you are too busy; you keep telling me I'm hard to live with."

"You're collecting negative signs of love. Do a real accounting and collect the positive signs of love. What about the time I made your favorite meal? And the time you were so upset I stayed up to talk to you. And the times I tell you how admirable you are? And while we're collecting these negative signs of love, has it ever occurred to you that you make me feel unloved too?" (List these.) "I am a good accountant and I tote up your signs of love because I remember...." (List the signs of love.)

Families where members are allowed to be who they are and are listened to without negative judgments will foster openness because there is no fear. Openness allows the freedom to think as myself and for myself; to be who I am as I am, to become all I can be. When this freedom exists, I can be open because I trust that no one is out to get me. What lies behind that freedom to be is being loved just as I am right now.

I may give the impression that we all communicate with great facility. We don't. We are thirteen individuals who communicate in thirteen different ways. Seven of us do so with ease. Four prefer to keep the cards close to the chest, although one is converting to the first group. One has trouble articulating what she really wants to say and another prefers to keep things light, never deep. We try to give one another space and the acceptance that will keep us from having to feel defensive. We try to create a climate where we can all bloom. We know this takes time, but we have all of our lives to achieve this. There are no deadlines to loving.

Open communication happens when—

1. we stop concealing thoughts and feelings from each other.
2. we are willing to explain what is bothering us.
3. we express our thoughts and feelings to the person concerned, not to someone else.
4. we are listened to.
5. we can speak our minds and hearts without being judged.
6. we realize that love has no deadlines.

Thank you, Rob and Father Bob!

CHAPTER XV

LISTENING INTO BEING

"To listen to someone," says Catherine Doherty, is "to listen him into being."

To instill values and good habits into our children, we forget that we must first learn who they are. How do they tick? What makes them tick? We are so concerned about having them listen to us that it doesn't occur to many of us to listen to them. Why is listening often set aside? Parents do not listen to their children; children do not listen to their parents. Co-parents do not listen to each other and neither do siblings. We are all transmitters without receivers. The basic stance seems to be "Listen; these are my expectations of you. Now live up to them. Yak, yak, yak...."

Where there is no listening, no contact is made and estrangement ensues. Where there *is* listening, intimacy happens and the child knows he is appreciated—grain and chaff together.

Do you study your child? Lillian Gilbreth's son, Frank, said of her that "she knew what each one of her twelve children wanted, needed, dreaded, and dreamed about." When a child talked to her, she listened and listened and made sure she understood. This is my ambition—to be the kind of mother Lillian Gilbreth was. An attitude I see in many adults says "You listen to me. I've lived longer and I know what's what." Underneath is that unspoken but unmistakable statement, "What do you know about anything?" I marvel that today many adults from my childhood still see me from that standpoint. This teaches me to be more sensitive to those younger than I.

Many young people say, "My parents don't really care about me. They yammer at me and tell me what they want me to do or be." Or "My parents don't like me." Or "They are not really interested in me." Parents often have dreams riding on their children. They saddle the children with the burden of making those dreams come true, never mind who they are. They expect athletes out of poets, scientists out of woodworkers, lawyers out of artists, elephants out of butterflies.

When Jack was nearly twenty-one, he said, "Mom, you and Dad must be disappointed in me because I seem to lack direction in my life. I see Pat (a close friend) getting a master's degree and what do I have to show for myself?"

"Jack, there is no deadline to becoming who God is calling you to be. All I want for you is that you do something you truly enjoy so that you are happy, that you keep a lively relationship with God all your life, and be a loving, giving person. That is all. However you work out the details is fine with me." When he was thirty-four, that's exactly what he did. Praise God! His friend, Pat Kilner, remarked, "Jack plays all day long!" That's because Jack was doing what he really loved doing—taking people on outdoor adventures like rock climbing and shooting the rapids.

Very often, children read a message from their parents that conveys in words, actions, and reactions "This is what I want you to be. Be that." What they really long to hear from their parents is "Tell me about yourself. What are your dreams? Can I help you make them come true? What are your fears and pains? May I help? What is life like for you?"

Of course, such conversations don't begin quite like that. One day, Gabe came over, quite put out with his mother. He was in his room cleaning when she came in and said, "Talk to me, Son. Talk to me." That infuriated him. He felt pushed into doing something he didn't want to do. Real conversations cannot readily be switched on and off. They happen. If you want someone to share their dreams with you, then share yours with them. Relationships grow from exchanges. If you do not share your fears and pains with someone, why should that person bring hers to you? When we open up to others, we invite them tacitly to open up to us. Gabe and his friend, Matt, often said they knew more about us than they did about their own parents.

My favorite lines about listening come from Paul Hinnebusch's chapter on "The Listening Father" in his book, *Community in the Lord*.

> A good father is ever a good listener, ever lovingly attentive to his child.... He listens throughout the years to hear all his [child's] needs.

He listens attentively to what his child is saying in his whole being and in all that he does....

He gives what needs to be given to the child, and he lovingly calls forth from him, by word and encouragement, what can grow only from within....

A father can lovingly call forth what is in the child only if he is lovingly attentive to the child to discern what is in him.... Thus, a father is not one who imposes his own arbitrary will upon his son, demanding obedience. He is one who first listens to his son's true needs, and then lovingly invites him, directs him, encourages him in accordance with these needs....

He learns what the child should be, not by studying himself, but by listening to all that is in the child.... The father does not impose himself upon the child, nor does he impose upon him any preconceived notions of what this child should be. He forms his idea of what the child should be by obeying what he finds in the child, namely, all the wonderful potentialities that God has placed there. He rejoices in the treasures he finds in the child, because God put them there to be lovingly nurtured and invited forth to full development.

A listening father, then, is one who recognizes his son. To appreciate someone is to recognize his value and rejoice in it with love. To appreciate a child means to reverence the child, for the value we recognize in him as a person is so sublime that it deserves nothing less than profound love and reverence.

All that we say about listening fathers is true, of course, about listening mothers and listening teachers. (Notre Dame, Indiana: Ave Maria Press, 1975, pp. 15-17)

Listening goes beyond hearing words. It is reading body language, discerning vibes, reading accurately between the lines, noticing the light or lack thereof in the person's eyes, the energy or the absence of it in the voice. It is listening with more than just one's ears; it is listening with all of one's senses and all of one's heart.

Clare was a young mother whose son, Kevin, trailed her around the house asking her if she loved him. She assured him that she did, but he kept right on asking. It was driving her crazy. I suggested that perhaps he kept asking her because her vibes and her words didn't match. Her words said, "I love you, Kevin," but her vibes said, "You're driving me crazy. Get away from me." I encouraged her to tell him how she felt so that he wouldn't be confused. Then, when he wasn't asking her, to tell him she loved him or just hug him when he wasn't expecting it. It worked.

Parents frequently don't listen to their children because they are too busy with incidentals. The children get the message that work or hobbies are more important to their parents. I am not advocating that parents drop whatever they're doing when a child clamors for attention. I am saying, however, that if your children and their development are not the most important things in your life, they will sense that. If they are important, they will know that, too, even if you tell them, "When I'm working on the bills, don't bother me!"

When my children, grandchildren, and students bug me, I tell them they bug me and give them the reason. I also tell them frequently that I love them. They do not see these as contradictions. It is sad when children think they will be loved only when they are completely acceptable. Love and honesty enable children to relax enough to be who they really are, to be open and free enough to take risks because they know they need not be perfect at all times to be loved. Children can do the same for us, too.

Over the years, my children have listened me into being. We often reflect together, and they reflect me back to me. Friends do this and it is especially rewarding when those friends are your children. If anyone knows my dark side, it is my children. Yet the mirror they hold up to me reflects someone who is lovable.

Several years ago, I wrote in my journal that I felt as if I were zero. One day, I noticed a piece of paper at that page. It said something to the effect that my zero put beside anyone increased that person's value by ten—and wasn't that wonderful. It wasn't signed, but I'm a good sleuth. I discovered it came from twelve-year-old Annie. The two of us do a great deal of reflecting together. She is so wise that my value increases after I talk to her. It always does when my children and I talk.

This is a good time to ask ourselves the following:

1. Do we listen others—especially our children—into being?
2. Do we know what our children want, need, dread, and dream about?
3. Do we have dreams riding on our children?
4. Do we reverence our children?
5. Do our children think they're the most important of all that we value?

6. Do they trust this enough to relax and really be who they are?
7. Do we know how our children see us?

Thank you, Annie!

CHAPTER XVI

HONESTLY!

Perhaps the best message for parents is this: It is possible to make every conceivable mistake a parent can make and still live to enjoy parenthood. I am living proof of this. All mistakes are learning opportunities. "That didn't work. Let's try something else." Benefit from the mistakes of others. Study the success stories. Keep evolving. Develop more creative ways of being. Do not get hooked into unproductive ways of dealing with misbehavior. Look at it as one big exciting puzzle!

This chapter traces my evolution from man-eating tigress with cubs who lied through their teeth to human mother whose children didn't speak with forked tongues. I was so formidable in dealing with our older children that they would lie rather than incur my wrath. The younger ones—for whatever reason—felt less need to lie. They may have discovered they could afford to tell the truth. I really would not devour them whole when they did something wrong. That's the blessing of having many children. You get several chances to clean up your act.

Lying

Kids lie because they want their cake and eat it too. They want to do something that could get them into trouble but without getting punished. Lying could do the trick. Or they might try something you disapprove of—drinking, for example—without losing your disapproval. We have to find a way to discourage the misbehavior without encouraging a lie.

One of my girls lied habitually. She'd get into trouble and then try to lie her way out of it. She'd get caught in the lie and then get into more trouble for the misdeed and the lie. I tried to explain to her that if she told the truth, she'd be in trouble for the misdeed only. "How many times have you lied and gotten away with it?"

"Never."

"So why do you keep lying?"

"I keep thinking maybe this time I won't get caught."

In the days when garbage bags were waxed brown paper, one evening I found the garbage in the middle of the floor. Apparently, the bottom had fallen off the bag as someone transported it to the trash can.

I used every trick in the book to get the culprit to admit the deed. One that worked well when popsicles disappeared was to promise a spanking for everyone. The popsicle "thief" couldn't bear to have the others punished unjustly on her account so she stepped forward. The garbage plopper, however, had no sensitive conscience.

I told them God was listening and knew when they were lying. "To lie to God is like spitting in his face," I said.

"Were you the one who dropped the garbage?" Garbage plopper wasn't impressed enough to say "Yes." I was stymied since I was sure who the culprit was and said so—the person who cleaned the kitchen that night, the habitual liar. I added that unless Culprit could prove otherwise by morning, Culprit would get it. But Papa stepped in and said the evidence was circumstantial and would not be admissible.

The next morning I announced that if the culprit owned up to the misdeed, there would be no spanking. So who comes breezing along but Suspect/Culprit announcing, "I just remembered. It was me!"

"Don't you dare tell another lie! A few minutes after you dropped the garbage, you forgot it was you? Now the minute I announce there will be no spanking, you suddenly remember? Go upstairs and fetch the crucifix."

Up she went and returned with the crucifix. Then I said, "Spit on it!" She was horrified. I went on, "When you spit on that, you are spitting on a metal corpus hanging on a wooden cross. Last night, you spat on the face of God." That was the last time my habitual liar lied to me.

Shoplifting

There are two main reasons for shoplifting. One is obvious: The shoplifter wants something he or she has no money for. The other is the thrill of doing something without getting caught. God blessed us—the four times our children shoplifted, they got caught. Praise God! Nothing nips a career in crime so efficiently as getting caught.

On one shoplifting spree, the shoplifter was about six. He came home with some candy after shopping with an older sister. In questioning him, we heard a manufactured story full of holes. When I pointed out the holes, he admitted he had shoplifted. Off to the store we went. I told him to go to the manager and tell the man what he had done. He went alone. The manager, God bless him, used the perfect balance of sternness—"You realize that the next time this happens I will have to call the police"—and kindness, "Ask your mother," he said gently, "for jobs she will pay you to do so you can pay me for the candy." Making them face the music worked every time. Confessing to a store manager takes all the fun out of shoplifting.

The other half of the shoplifting story is the preventive half. When they asked to go to the store to purchase something, I was both specific and emphatic: "It will take you a minute to find the notebooks, another minute to make your selections. It should take another five minutes to pay for it. Be back in ten minutes." That left them no time to get tempted—we live next door to the drugstore.

Finders, keepers

Tom found ten dollars when he walked through the Baptist Church parking lot. We talked it over; I suggested that he write a note to the pastor and enclose the ten dollars. After all, if that were his money wouldn't he appreciate it if someone turned it in? Tom sent the note and the money to the pastor who, God bless him, wrote Tom the loveliest note praising him for his honesty. It is people like the store manager and the pastor who help us greatly as we steer our children past the potholes and the open manholes of growing up today.

Honesty

Sister Kathleen called. Rob had threatened a child on the playground. As soon as Rob walked in, I met him with "What's this I hear about you and the Dowling boy?"

"Mom, what would you do if someone kept aggravating you, you asked them to stop, but they kept it up?" He made no attempt to deny anything or whitewash the problem. I counted it progress that my last child no longer needed to lie to me. But I'm not sure it had anything to do with me. Rob was never one of the cake-eater keepers. He was always willing to accept the consequence of his choices. And proud as I was of him for not lying, I still had to play Sermon Twenty-three: "Being kind to others."

These are the lessons I learned:

1. Tone down your reactions to the children's misdeeds so that they will be willing to confess the truth.
2. Prevent shoplifting by monitoring trips to the store.
3. Praise them when they show integrity.

Thank you, Tom!
Thank you, Rob!

CHAPTER XVII

BEING KIND TO OTHERS

If my kids could possess only one virtue, I would choose kindness. Never mind the rest. I have a suspicion that all other virtues follow if a person is kind, for kindness springs from love.

Can one teach kindness? I think so. I am not a naturally kind person, but with God's grace, persistent effort and by modeling kind people, I am learning. If I can learn, so can my children.

How is kindness taught? It begins with thinking of others instead of one's self only, putting the other's comfort before one's own. Bruce Larson calls it being a host instead of a guest. To teach kindness to children, make them aware of the other person and that person's needs. Point out the kind things people do for people; invite them to give of themselves.

I am not sure how we did this but casual suggestions helped. "Chris, please help Bim make her bed." "Chip, see if Mrs. Keller needs her walk shoveled." "Rob, why don't you carry that lady's grocery bag home for her."

Help the children see others as persons. "I hate Mrs. Lowell; she's a terrible teacher. She's so grouchy."

"Maybe she's not feeling well. Why don't you ask her if she's feeling okay."

I always asked for their help: "Kids, I barely slept a wink last night—the baby was sick. Will you take over so I can take a nap?" Often, they were understanding and gracious. When they weren't, I tried to make them understand and be gracious. My children learned that a sleepless mother is like ten raging tigresses.

Many years later—maybe fifteen—I came home from work dead tired. The "baby" took one look at me and said, "You look so tired."

"I am. I corrected papers all night."

"Take a nap, Mom. I'll fix dinner." It took! That is kindness.

One of my happiest moments happened on Cape Cod in 1969. We were at a laundromat doing the laundry for thirteen people. As we waited, we watched other people with their laundry. One woman had several baskets of clothes and a box with laundry detergent and bleach. It would have taken several trips to her car. As she headed for the door, Chrissy got up and, without a word, carried out a basket. Her siblings saw her and followed suit. When the woman reached her car, she saw this parade of munchkins following her. I was so proud of them because the gesture came from the goodness of their own hearts. I hadn't prompted them.

We are blessed with many kind people in our lives. We can point them out to our children as models for kindness. Our neighbors in the two neighborhoods where we've lived were very good to us. At Jennings Court, I had had a miscarriage. Friends and neighbors came in, cleaned the house, took care of the children, brought meals, did the laundry. When Papa got sick last year, again we experienced love and kindness and goodness. Rob said, "Mom, we are covered with so much love and so many prayers that even if we wanted to fall down we wouldn't be able to; the love and prayers would hold us up." Praise God for such friends!

Our extended family is outstanding in generosity. We practice pure communism as it is described in Acts: from each according to his capacity, to each according to his need. My bachelor uncle, Lolo Dado, sent the children and us on trips abroad, gave them cars, bought us appliances and furniture. He was our family's fairy godfather. My sisters are fairy godmothers and we have fairy grandparents, great aunts, and great uncles. It would take a book to recount these gifts.

Friends, neighbors, and relatives give us so much of their time, resources, energies, and themselves. The children, no doubt, have grown up believing there is no other way to be.

Then there is compassion. If kindness means walking a mile in another person's moccasins, compassion goes even further. It is living inside his/her skin, seeing the world through his/her eyes. I'll always remember an episode in Star Trek when an entity enters a human body and says, "Oh, my, it is so lonely in here." If we could do that, we would be less apt to judge others because we would understand their pain. Can we teach our children this? A child would say, "How do you get inside another person's skin?" My answer: "Be interested in them, find out what they are thinking and feeling, try to see what they see." Then it becomes a game—take the spotlight off self and focus it on others.

Did my children balk at sharing? Did they fight over toys? Of course they did. When I was lamenting about one of my children's latest escapades, Doris Murray said, "Why should your children be different from ours?"

I always had the same solution to this fighting-over-something bit: "If you fight over it, I'll take it away and neither of you can have it." They had two choices: lose the thing altogether or take turns with it. They made the decision. Either way, the fighting stops. This works even with two year olds.

This one works well if they have a concept of time: My grandson, Ben, had a ball his sister, Sarah, coveted. She said, "He won't share."

"Tell you what, Sarah. Let him play with it for ten minutes and then you can have it. Okay, Ben?" They both assented. At the end of ten minutes neither of them was interested in the ball.

Another time, one of my kids walked in with a cookie a neighbor had given him. Little sibling wanted a bite. Have didn't want to share with Have Not. Have Not was devastated. I held the cookie between them and said to Have, "You don't want to give him a bite because a whole cookie is better than a half. Right?"

"Yup!"

Addressing Have Not, I said, "You would like half because half is better than none. Right?"

"Uh-huh."

Turning to Have, I continued, "Suppose this cookie belonged to your brother instead of you. What would you want him to do?"

"Give me half."

"But since it's yours, what will you do?"

"Give him half." He walked a little way in his brother's shoes, understood, and freely made the kind decision.

We can teach our children kindness by helping them learn how to walk a mile in other people's moccasins, helping them see others as persons, inviting them to give of themselves. We can point out to them the good things people do for others so that they will have role models in kindness. We can help them see how and why sharing with others benefits them, too. We can work especially at being kind ourselves.

So much for sharing possessions. What about sharing responsibility? That's our next chapter.

Thank you, Lolo Dado!
Thank you, fairy godfamily and fairy godfriends!
Thank you, role models in kindness!
Thank you, Chrissy and Munchkins!

CHAPTER XVIII

THE PIE

How do you get an unwilling child to assume his share of responsibility around the house?

As a child moves from babyhood into childhood, he asserts himself more and more. At about age seven, the game goes like this.
"Brian, please pick up those clothes on the floor."
"They're not mine. Why should I pick them up?"
"Brian, why didn't you clear the rest of the table?"
"Those aren't my plates. Why should I?"
This kind of response goes on all day long.
Next day, suppertime rolls around; there's no place set for Brian. Everyone but Brian gets served. "Hey, where's my plate? What's going on? How come I didn't get served?"
"I'm not going to swallow your food so I didn't cook any for you. Make your own supper."
Brian goes to get his laundry. His unwashed clothes are still on the floor. "Why aren't my clothes washed?"
"I don't wear them. Why should I wash them?"
Several more instances like this happen and Brian doesn't like it. "That's not fair," he says.
"Hey, Brian, these are your rules. Remember? My rule is 'All for one and one for all.' Take care of everybody and everybody takes care of you. Your rule is 'Brian is only for Brian.' Make your choice. You can't have it both ways where you take care of no one and everyone takes care of you. You tell me which system you want and we'll go with your decision."
For a few days, Brian is out to prove he can go it alone until he

gets tired of washing his own clothes, eating peanut butter sandwiches, and begging for paid chores so he can pay for his own hot lunch at school. No sermon could teach him more poignantly about community, solidarity, and isolation.

All this takes time and energy, but so does purposeless hassling. The point to all of these tactics is to help the child see the ramifications of his selfishness, thoughtlessness, and immaturity. Incidentally, there are two adjectives young people prize highly describing qualities they will do anything to earn: cool and mature. Therefore, they have motivating value. When you come right down to it, parenting is teaching. We simply have to keep teaching as long as it takes children to learn. Some children need only one lesson to get the point. Others take more.

How early should you get children to help with chores?

When a child is about three, she is eager to help around the house. A job is a badge of maturity. When you have a job, you are no longer a baby. You're one of the big guys! In our family, the first chore was to take the milk bottles to the milk box on the porch. (That dates us, doesn't it?) Our children began to do that on their third birthday.

At three, a child begs to work: wash dishes, wipe the table, sweep the floor, wash the walls. Name the chore, she wants to do it. I say, "Let her." By the time she realizes it's work and not fun, it will have become a habit.

My friend, Tina, said, "I don't want Diana in the kitchen to mess it up. She can learn to cook and do other chores when she has her own home." Like Diana, I learned on my own. When we were first married, I vividly remember standing before the stove, weeping with frustration. It was then I vowed I would never raise children as inept as I was.

My grandmother really intended that I learn how to work in the kitchen. She would say, "Honey, go to the kitchen and help Yaya Bating (the cook)." I'd go into the kitchen; Yaya would ask me to chop onions, slice meat, or do some such task. But between chattering endlessly and being a klutz, I drove Yaya to distraction. Very sweetly she would say, "Inday, do you really want to help me?"

"Oh, yes!"

"Then why don't you go outside and play?" Yaya Bating mirrored Tina: better a dumb kid than a disorganized kitchen or a haphazard meal.

But with my experience, it was the other way around—better a chaotic kitchen and "unusual" meals than unprepared kids. Papa is the real hero for he ate many bizarre meals. The upshot is that all eleven are great cooks!

What if they refuse to shoulder their share of the load?

Every now and then someone decides to balk and sloughs off doing her share of the job. At that time we trot out Sermon Nine, "The Pie." I draw a pie with thirteen pieces and put everyone's name on the slices. The pie stands for family responsibilities. Each of us has one-thirteenth of the whole according to our abilities. Obviously, the baby's one-thirteenth is not the same as Papa's. When someone doesn't want to carry his share, then his one-thirteenth has to be divvied up among the remaining twelve. Someone else says, "If she can slough hers off, why can't I?" He does, and his share is again divvied up among the remaining eleven. Then another says, "I don't want to carry mine either." Again, we divide hers among the remaining ten. This goes on until one day, only one person is left carrying thirteen-thirteenths.

At this point, I pull myself up to my full five-feet, two-inch height, tower over the balker with the "glare," and snarl, "How would you like to be that someone?" The balker looks at the one-thirteenth slice that is hers and the thirteen-thirteenths that could be hers and decides she has a pretty good deal after all.

What if they think they have more to do than the others?

On the last day of school in June, I would make a huge, elaborate, color-coded chart assigning chores to everyone. Blue for personal tasks such as making one's own bed, red for family chores such as dishwashing, green for child care such as feeding one of the little ones, and yellow for leisure time. They could see for themselves that they had equal shares of leisure periods. Friends asked why I wasted so much time doing the complicated chart. For one reason, it simplified my yelling. Instead of saying, "Chris, do this! Bim, do that! Jack, this! Nini, that!" I simply bellowed, "Look at your schedules!" It was scientific, systematic, well-balanced, fair, and quite colorful. I am not a systems analyst's wife for nothing.

Even the little ones who didn't know how to read got schedules. I drew pictures of their chores instead of writing them: a bed for making their beds, a broom for sweeping their rooms, a toothbrush for brushing their teeth, etc. Having their own schedules made them feel grown-up and they loved checking off their schedules just like the "big guys."

How to assign the chores—by ability and/or preference?

Each child had his/her day to cook, clean, do laundry. They would have preferred, of course, to do the jobs they enjoyed. Chrissy, for example, loved to cook and hated the laundry. But that was not the point. I wanted each of them to be proficient in every task. Dorothy Canfield Fisher said, "Mothers are to make leaning unnecessary." I wanted to raise our kids to be so self-sufficient that if I died, their lives could go on without a skip. I also read somewhere that good parents are those who work themselves out of a job. That was my goal.

Are some chores just for boys and others just for girls?

Once I asked a child from a big family if he cooked. Surprised, he said, "Cooking is girl's work." I told him I didn't know work had sexes. Our boys and girls cooked, sewed, did the laundry, chopped wood, cared for babies, built furniture. "Anything anyone can do, I can do," was the guideline. Thanks to the grace of God, I think I have fulfilled my vow not to raise children as inept as I was.

Were your children always self-sufficient?

Hah! Some had to be coerced. My friend, Emilia, once remarked, "Do you realize that your older children are more self-sufficient than your younger ones? The younger ones are used to being taken care of by your older ones."

I hadn't noticed. But the next day was Sunday. At about eight o'clock I said, "All right, everybody, time to get ready to go to church!" Joe, then about three or four, went up the stairs. When he got to the top, he stretched out his arms and said, "Somebody change me!" I charged up the stairs and threatened, "Don't anybody touch him. All right, young man, change yourself—by yourself!"

Then there was Mecky. The family says she raised herself. She always did everything before it was time; consequently, she was born with teeth, stood up at six months, walked at ten months, toilet-trained herself. She was self-motivated from conception on.

To help children realize that family life is a community affair:

1. Help them see the advantages of "all for one and one for all" as compared with "I am only for me."
2. Let them help when they're little and think work is fun. By the time they realize it isn't, it will have become a habit.
3. Let them see that everyone else is contributing and recognize what would happen if everyone balked.
4. Teach them the skills they will need to be self-sufficient. "Mothers are to make leaning unnecessary." (Dorothy C. Fisher)
5. Parenting is basically teaching; keep teaching until the children learn the lessons. Teaching involves motivation—motivating with a purpose is much better than purposeless hassling.

Thank you, Mecky!

CHAPTER XIX

WHAT ABOUT OBEDIENCE?

There are times these days when people seem to consider obedience as a dirty word. Really, obedience is a marvelous boon to parents. For centuries—and even today in some parts of the world—obedience is still a value. A child learns obedience and no one apologizes for it.

When you tell your toddler to stay out of the street, you value obedience. When you tell him not to wander off in a store, you prize obedience. When you tell her to sit still in a restaurant, you appreciate obedience. Why, then, are many parents loathe to make their children obey?

I suspect it is because it means pitting wills with someone half your size but standing a good chance of losing the battle. Some years ago, Connor and Cameron spent every Tuesday with me. At first, they didn't always come when I called them. That was new to me. However, I simply made them understand my expectations; now they come.

As I write this, my oldest child is thirty-six and my youngest is twenty-one. I haven't pitted wills with any of them for some time, but I baby-sit with the grandchildren and I wonder whether my expectations are still valid. This is a good time to find out! Two-year-old Eddie is getting cross. "Eddie, it's time for your nap."

"I don't want to take a nap!"

"I didn't ask you if you wanted to take a nap, Ed," I answer gently but firmly. "You are going to take a nap because you're cross; that means you're tired." I take him by the hand and we go upstairs without a battle. It still works—and I didn't even raise my voice!

When children ask "Why?" I explain. "I don't want you to run out into the street because a car might hit you and hurt you; I love you so much and I don't want that to happen to you." If I see the child cannot be trusted, I don't leave him without supervision. I work on the premise that clarity of purpose encourages cooperation. "Because I said so," is a cop-out that doesn't work.

Perhaps another reason parents today are reluctant to make their children obey is their fear of repressing them. It all depends on your reasons for making your children obedient. Do you want to be in control and get them to do and be what you want? Telling a child to take a nap so he won't be too tired to see a play in the evening is hardly repressive.

It is possible to have obedient children who are free, self-motivated, unrepressed, fully human persons. I can say that because we have raised eleven of them. Children who have strong-minded parents tend to become well-boundaried, less repressed. They had to define early in life who they were to survive their formidable parents. However, this holds true only if the parents are not interested in absorbing their children and see them as having the right to be who they are as individuals.

What happens when children disobey? We have an oft-quoted saying in our house: "In life there are neither rewards nor punishments, only consequences."

There are set "consequences" for specific breaches in behavior. If you have not done your chores, you may not go out with your friends. If you throw a fit, you get Sermon Ten. It goes like this:

"Right now you are acting like the cuckoo who wanted to go north but boarded the bus that goes south instead because he didn't want to cross the street to catch the northbound bus. You're throwing a fit because the bus didn't go where you wanted it to go when you knew full well where it was going. Or you are like the nincompoop who wanted some cold water. You turned on the hot water faucet and got upset because the hot water came out. In other words, my Dear, if you want to go north, take the northbound bus! If you want cold water, turn on the cold water faucet! If you want to go out with your friends, do your chores. If you don't want to do your chores, don't expect to be allowed to go out. It's that simple!

"At the end of every misbehavior is an unpleasant consequence. At the end of every positive behavior is a pleasant consequence. When you choose the behavior, you choose the consequence. I only promise to deliver the consequence that goes with the behavior you have chosen—without fail and every time!"

Many times I felt sorry for them, but I didn't let that sway me; for I believe pity only weakens. Jack got an "A" that he had struggled for. We gave him ten dollars as a "pleasant consequence." At that time, the children were selling Holy Childhood seals for school. Jack wanted a particular prize and he could get it if he sold ten dollars worth of seals. I suggested he bring home one set of seals at a time to minimize the risk of misplacing them. But no! He brought all ten booklets home, each worth a dollar. He left them in his pants pocket and they got laundered. There went the ten dollars for his "A." I wanted so much to pay for the seals because I felt sorry for him but—being La Verduga—I didn't. "In life," I intoned, "there are neither rewards nor punishments, only consequences." It was a learning experience.

Kids, as a matter of course, try to push your buttons or, in today's parlance, manipulate you. If they sense that you feel guilty, they will lay guilt trips on you. If they perceive you as having a public persona and a private one, they will do things in public they wouldn't dare do in private. They know you won't make a scene in front of others. When mine did that, I took them to the nearest rest room and said between gritted teeth, "If you don't care enough about me to spare me public embarrassment, I don't care that much for you either. The next time you publicly embarrass me, I shall publicly chastise you. Do you understand? If you don't believe me, try me." One tried it. When the people around me got wide-eyed at my response to the child, I told them I had promised her that. "I told her that if she kept interrupting me in public when I was talking, I'd tap her on the mouth. She did. So I did!"

The trick to the obedience game is looking for and finding the magic "Open sesame!" that will unlock a child's willingness to cooperate. Teaching obedience is not intended to manufacture androids programmed to be exactly who we want them to be. Rather, it serves to motivate children to learn how to make felicitous choices: wise and mature, loving and kind, noble and gracious, unselfish and freeing.

Obedience is a marvelous boon to parents. It comes more easily when—

1. we explain the reasons behind our requests.
2. our requests are reasonable, logical, and have nothing to do with our need to assert power over them.

3. we understand that obedience does not mean repression.
4. we and the children understand that "in life there are neither rewards nor punishments, only consequences."
5. we understand that obedience teaches the child how to make happier choices.

Thank you Connor, Cameron, and Eddie!

CHAPTER XX

"MOM IS CULTURING US!"

The phone rang while we were having dinner; twelve-year-old Rob got up to answer it. "Can I call you back later?" he said to the caller. "Mom is culturing us right now." No, I wasn't making human yogurt. We were playing a dinner table game. They would give me a category, I'd ask a question in the category, and they had to answer it. For example, Nini would say, "Science." I'd ask, "Who was Lister?" Or Rob might say, "Art." I'd ask, "Who painted the ceiling of the Sistine Chapel?" No big deal; just fun.

When I was growing up during World War II, we often didn't have school and there was nothing to do. So Neng and I prowled around looking for things to do at our uncle, Papa Nene's house. He had many books including the Harvard Classics. We began with the *Fairy Tales* volume. We read that volume so much that it is a shade lighter than the other volumes. When we practically memorized that one, we moved on like steamrollers to *Arabian Nights, The Knights of the Round Table, Robin Hood*. There was no stopping us.

Papa Nene noticed all this and was delighted. At the dinner table, he'd ask, "Have you read *The Talisman* yet?" No. He then proceeded to tell us about it. We hung on to his every word and if he paused, we prompted, "Then what?" "Read the book and find out for yourself." He did this repeatedly with book after book after book.

I was ten years old and Neng was eight. Papa Nene taught us how to type, do architectural drawings, and write poems. Shakespeare was his passion. After the war, he bought all the Shakespearean records he could find and played them for his pleasure and our benefit. We sat in his study committing to memory what we heard, much the way kids memorize commercials today.

COMPOST MAKES THE STRAWBERRIES GROW

As my children came along, I taped Laurence Olivier's "Once more unto the breach" speech from *Henry V* so our children could enjoy what I did as a child. By the time he was five, Tom could recite it with all of Olivier's inflections and cadences, but with some minor variations: "Once more unto the breach, dear friends, once more! Or close the wall up INTO our English dead!"

I tried to bribe them. I promised them ten dollars if they would memorize a soliloquy from Hamlet. Gene Ahern thought that was a rash offer. I didn't have to pay it until Rob went to college. All the others got stuck on the tenth line. Emily, Jack's ten-year-old daughter, is working on it.

Nay Alicia, a maternal aunt, did not want to send her children, Doreen, Della, and Nil away to the good schools in Manila. She wanted her children at home with her and their father. So she taught them, using the Calvert School Home Program. Whatever Doreen and Della read, Neng and I read. She kept her children's books on Greek and Roman mythology and art next to their comic books. On Sunday afternoons, we devoured the books on the classics, comics, literature, and art. She kept classical records with Mother Goose records, operas, operettas, and musicals. We played them all. We had no idea she was culturing us!

When I got to college, I discovered that those "stories" from my childhood were *The Iliad and the Odyssey*! I promised myself then that I would try to do the same for the children I would have some day. We have tried to do this, but I am not sure all of our children are as cultured as I would like them to be. There is still free will. At best, we can culture them surreptitiously and be content with whatever rubs off. Some, like Chrissy, are better encyclopedias than others.

Now that she has five children of her own, Chrissy is merrily culturing them. On her dining room wall she has a list of countries and their capitals (Amy knew them by heart at five), the Periodic Table, maps, and the genealogy of the biblical patriarchs. She had large-sized flash cards, 1+1=2, for Andrew when he was three. On a slate in the living room they write the word for the day. The day we visited, it was "mausoleum." Like her, Charlie and Rachel go through books like little termites.

When I was fourteen, we went to live with our aunt, Manang Purit, who founded the Art Association of the Philippines. She exposed us to art. The leading artists of the country would leave their paintings at the house before an exhibit and Manang Purit would call our attention to the various things to look for in a painting. I absorbed all of this and have tried to pass it on to our children.

One summer I required the children to keep notebooks. Every day I'd give them new words. They had to find the meanings and then use them in sentences. I gave them names of famous people. They had to find out who they were. They had to draw in those notebooks and write poems and stories. Papa felt sorry for them. He thought vacation time should be just that—vacation time. Chrissy, today, makes the preposterous claim that I made her read a condensed version of Aquinas's *Summa Theologica* when she was ten!

Some years ago, when Jeni and Jessie stayed with us for a week during the summer, I got them notebooks. They loved doing them. Culturing is fun!

Several of the children took piano lessons, courtesy of Lala, Papa's mother. But they ended up guitar players. When Gene Ahern went to France in 1967, he left his guitar with us. He told the kids that if they learned to play it by the time he returned, it was theirs. I taught them the three chords I knew, and we sang twenty-two songs with those three chords. They went on to learn all the chords and the songs they wanted to sing.

We played different kinds of music. Our music: classical, opera, Philippine; their music: folk and rock; and the music we all had in common: Broadway musicals. One of my greatest pleasures was to discover that Connor and Cameron loved *La Boheme.*

If we surround our children with richness, they will absorb it subconsciously and enjoy it. We don't need to structure it. Culture is more fun when it is insidious.

If I came from my childhood bearing books and records, Papa brought into our life together an abundance of solid, tangible, visible, and useful skills and craftsmanship. Our children have inherited the talents and have gone on to use them in new ways.

Lala was born in the Ozarks. She grew up on a farm where she learned to cook, can, sew, knit, crochet, tat, quilt, garden, make preserves. You name it, she did it—with great gusto. She taught those things to us and our children.

When Lolo, Papa's father, retired, he went into lapidary work, making beautiful rings and pins. Because they always did things together, Lala, too, was a lapidarian, and was known as the gem lady in Colonial Beach, Virginia. Lala's father was a cabinetmaker. We have a few pieces of furniture that Papa made. He is proudest of the dining room table Doug Powell taught him to make and the blanket chest he helped Ben Bowling make.

Papa gardens, tools leather, supports the photo industry single-handedly with help from his camera-happy offspring. Lolo's father was a constabulary officer from a fishing village, and two of Papa's favorite pastimes are hunting and fishing. All of his genes and chromosomes seem operative, and the good things he inherited are bearing fruit, enjoyed and passed on through the generations.

All of the children garden. Their love of the land stems from all sides of the family. They cook well; the girls are creative with needles, sewing, knitting, crocheting, and embroidering. The boys are handy with tools and can build whatever they want.

This happened without structure, without deliberate intention. When the children were little, they wanted to give each other Christmas presents but didn't have the money to express their generosity. Thus began the custom of making each other presents. The older girls would get pairless socks and make pretty dolls. The boys made spoons out of wood from the woodpile. In my impractical way, I wrote poems for gifts and they returned the favor. One Christmas, Annie made gingerbread houses for her married siblings.

The pattern continues. Chrissy makes beautiful banners, crochets Christmas ornaments, makes pysanky eggs. John, her husband, is a skilled photographer. Bim wins ribbons at county fairs for her knitting and the wool she spins, draws portraits, does water colors and flower arrangements. Robert, her husband, does fine woodwork and smiths. Jack built his wife, Terry, a lovely chest one Christmas but his main artwork is with people. Terry knits the menfolk socks and one year made each family a calendar noting all the birthdays and anniversaries. Nini knits and sews and embroiders; her husband, Jim, is a deft cartoonist. Mecky sews anything, makes wreaths and dolls and does other crafts. Phil made booster chairs for the grandchildren one Christmas.

Tom made us shelves and beautifies our houses. Jeannie is an aerobic teacher. Joe's photographs are welcome gifts, and Theresa sews and does calligraphy skillfully with Joe. She also "makes rooms," as her children proudly announce. Ann draws, works on calligraphy, sews, knits, and quilts. Chris, her husband, has a super green thumb, is a master cake baker and salad maker. Mary takes stunning photographs, makes bead earrings, embroiders, and cuts hair. Chip sculpts, draws, and makes interesting ceramic pieces. Rob is our writer and another poet—there are eight others—who also draws and keeps everything shipshape.

Here Tom was afraid that if you sat on the kids too much it would dampen their creativity! I haven't even mentioned their dancing or athletic prowess! One of the projects we talk about but haven't realized is a family crafts fair. We've just been too busy increasing the tribe.

Over the years, we have simply been surfacing gifts. People remark, "Your children are so gifted!" But isn't everybody's children? Isn't it our job to uncover all the wonderful things our children are?

I remarked to a neighbor whose daughter, a quiet girl I hadn't noticed much before, seemed to bloom suddenly, "Was your daughter always so gifted?" To my surprise, the woman replied, "I didn't even know she had those talents." The girl was in high school! The person who recognized her talents was our assistant pastor, Fr. Bob Mordino. His talent is to surface the talents of others. He is so good at this that one year we named him "mother of the year" on Mother's Day. He truly helped our children discover how wonderful they are.

One of the "funnest" parts of parenting is to discover the gifts a child has in store for the world to enjoy. Family life is like carefully tilled soil. A child grows, sunned by cherishing, fertilized by every conceivable enrichment, watered by loving interaction. The only possible result is a bountiful harvest of fruit.

To reiterate, this can all happen without extra lessons—we couldn't afford them—structured time, a punishing schedule, pressure, or stress. It happens by simply doing what comes "natcherly." As "natcherly" as "Our nativity figures are broken. Let's make our own. Each one makes a figurine. Take your pick." You should see that nativity set. It's hilarious!

When you ask children to do or make something, show them how, let them do the work without your supervision, but encourage them in their efforts. They will blossom and bloom and bring their particular gifts to completion.

Does this also apply to academic achievement? I think so. We didn't make grades an issue. The motivated ones motivated themselves. One day after they received report cards, Rob walked in bent out of shape because he had a B. In saunters Chip. "What about you, Chip?"

"I've got one of every letter!"

"You have an F?"

"No, not that one." He hands me his report card.

"You've got a D in math?"
"Hey, Ma, that's not an F!"
"You've got a C in science?"
"That's not a D!"
"You've got a B in English?"
"That's not a C!"
"Why is your math grade so low?"
"I don't understand what we're doing right now."
"What are you going to do about it?"
"I've made an appointment with my teacher and Mike is going to tutor me."
"Good. I trust it won't be a D next time then."
"Okay, Mom. It won't be."

When Chip was a senior in high school he made first honors.

I am often surprised how often parents expect their C children to deliver straight A's. Don't they know their child cannot do that? Why don't they? They have known her longer. They have looked at her but have never seen her. Then there are the parents who have the unmotivated A child. I would leave her alone and let her live with the consequences. Sometimes children use their grades to get back at their parents whose pressures they resent. I wouldn't give them the satisfaction.

Perhaps one reason parents make such an issue of grades is because they think conscientious parents should do that—push their children into achieving. There is only one hitch to that: It doesn't often work. It just creates pressure for the children and frustration for the parents. Find out why they are doing poorly, have them suggest solutions, and encourage them. The rest is in their own hands—and God's. We are their cheerleaders, not their Svengalis.

Too often parents decide the child's career and proceed to pound the child into a mold of parental ambitions. It is much easier, more fun, more gratifying and exciting to discover who, in truth, the child is. Then we can spend the rest of our lives digging up the gold within and be rich with it!

We culture our children when we—

1. surround them with richness so that they can absorb it unconsciously and enjoy it.
2. pass on to them the skills we have, leaving them to do their thing without supervising them.

3. surface their gifts and encourage their efforts.
4. create a climate at home that will allow them to blossom, bloom, and bring their gifts to fruition.

Thank you, Popsy, Pa Nene, Nay Alicia, and Manang Purit!
Thank you, Lolo and Lala!
Thank you, Gene Ahern and Father Mordino!
Thank you, Doug and Ben!
Thank you, Family!

THE SYSTEMS

CHAPTER XXI

FUSION VS. INTIMACY

Do you consider togetherness a great good? So did I. But there were times when I wasn't sure it was that good. I refer to those times when I was expected to change my plans and drop everything because my significant other wanted to do something else. When my feet dragging was evident, I was accused of being too individualistic and against the common good.

I have also been expected to think as many others think, say what they think I should say, and value their values. When I was a child, it seemed to surprise the grown-ups that I had ideas of my own. They often asked—and still do—"Why didn't you do this?" I didn't know there was a script. No one ever gave me one.

Much to my relief, I finally learned that togetherness, like people, can be good or bad. When it's good, it is called intimacy and is one of the deepest satisfactions a person can experience. Bad togetherness is fusion defined as an "undifferentiated ego mass." The first time I heard that in class I thought Father Walsh said, "undifferentiated ego mess." I began to laugh but no one else was laughing. I was so embarrassed. "I'm sorry, Father," I said, "I thought you said 'ego mess.'"

"That," he said, "is exactly what it is: a mess of egos."

Fused family members are like drops of water. Have you ever watched two drops of water, maybe on a leaf, come close to each other and suddenly, thlup! They become one big drop and you can't tell where the original, individual drops are. That's fusion. But put two marbles side by side for a century and they will still be two marbles side by side. They will never "thlup" each other. That's intimacy.

In unfused families, the members have a sense of who each is. They know where one ends and the other begins. In fused families, it's one big tangled hodgepodge of selves, and members don't differentiate one from the other. In every family there is usually a strong personality. In unfused families, this personality either doesn't attempt to absorb the others or the others are so well boundaried that they can't be absorbed. In fused families, this strong personality absorbs the others.

Fusion is so fraught with tension and is so uncomfortable that those involved will resort to one or all three ways to unfuse themselves; that is, conflict, dysfunctioning, and distancing.

Conflict is self-explanatory. It's simply out-and-out fighting.

Dysfunctioning finds the individual suffering so much from the fusion that he or she dysfunctions—breaks down. This includes all forms of substance abuse, physical, emotional, and mental illness.

Distancing puts actual or psychic distance between oneself and those one is fused with. This includes infidelity, workaholism, and noncommunication.

Another dynamic operative in fused families is triangling. Triangling happens when two parties do a togetherness against a third party. Mom and Dad do a togetherness against one child or all of the children. One parent does a togetherness with the children against the other parent. Or the parents do a togetherness with one youngster against another. We call this taking sides. It causes world wars and it can happen in your family. It did in ours until we took Father Walsh's course. Praise God!

There are two ways to deal with triangles. The first is to simply step out of it. When Papa and any of the youngsters did not see eye to eye on something, I volunteered to explain Papa's point of view to them and their point of view to Papa. After Father Walsh's course, I merely said to them, "You've got mouths, talk to each other. You've got ears, listen to each other." Then I left the room. That worked.

The second way to break up a triangle is for the odd one to affirm the togetherness of the other two. Father Walsh used this example: "If your husband has a romantic interest in someone else, tell him you're glad he found someone who makes him happy and understands him so well. Then suggest that he see her oftener." It sounds wild and weird but, astonishingly, reverse psychology is effective.

The last dynamic Father Walsh gave us was to have no secrets. This discourages concealment and miscommunication. If we have something to say to anyone, say it to the person concerned, not secretly to someone else. Direct communication eliminates much misunderstanding.

Learning these tactics helped us change many ways we related to one another. We looked for signs of fusion to discover what lay beneath the symptoms. Were we having too many fights? Was I lumping the kids into one corporate entity called the children? Did they look at us as the parents? We tried to define our boundaries as persons and helped the children define theirs. When they went through the motions of defining their boundaries, we realized that their apparent teenage rebellion was not necessarily directed at us personally. We stepped out of our triangles. We never were for secrets and this was affirming. It became easier for us as our children moved into young adulthood.

No one is really taught how to be a parent. For most of us, the only school for parenthood is the way we were parented. Some of us copy our parents to the tee, and we expect our children to respond to us just as we responded to our parents. If our parents monitored our friendships, we try to monitor our children's. If we accepted this, then we expect our children to react in the same way. If we considered our curfews too strict, we will likely not impose any on our children.

Parents need to give careful thought to what they do and to whom. Our children may be quite different from us and what worked with us may not work with them. We have to find the key that unlocks the best in each of our children. There will be as many keys as there are individuals.

Understanding all that goes into fusion and intimacy, triangles and secrets, enabled us to step out of the traps we could have locked ourselves into. It allowed us to move into relationships where we are close and free.

Thank you, Father Walsh!

CHAPTER XXII

WILL THEY KEEP OUR VALUES?

While attending a series of talks and discussions on adolescent behavior at one of our children's schools, I met the principal.

"What are you doing here?" he asked. "You could be giving this course."

"Oh, thank you! But you know, you can raise several children and think you know what's going on. The next one comes along and you discover you know nothing!"

I often think God made some children just to keep their parents from getting cocky. He happily interspersed our brood with such as these. Some of our kids are pats on the back to encourage us. Others keep us on our knees. It makes for a great balance.

When Jesus said, "Prophets are without honor in their own country," he must have had parents in mind. My students will accept from me what they reject from their parents. They ask me if my children accept what I teach. I admit that I have the credibility of a turnip with some of my children. Actually, it depends on the age. The older they are, the more credibility I have. Borrowing from Mark Twain, it's amazing how much smarter I got from the time my children were in their teens until they hit their twenties.

I have had two kinds of children: those who think I'm sensible and listen to me and the others who think I'm silly and ignore me. Recently, I discovered there is yet a third. Chip said, "Ma, I listen to you; I just can't give you the satisfaction."

Have you noticed how these tendencies are discernible very early? Little Miss Agreeable crawls toward the hot oven. "Don't touch it, Honey," you call out, "it's hot and you'll get hurt!" or words like "No! No! Hot!" She looks at you as if she were thinking, "She loves me and doesn't want me to get hurt. She's older and knows more than I do. I'll go along." She crawls away.

With Little Miss Resistant, the scenario begins the same way, the same admonition. She looks at you and her eyes read, "Maybe you got burned, but I'm not you." Hands onto the stove. Bawl. "Espiritu de contradiccion" is the term the Spanish have for those who have the compulsion to oppose. Their motto is "Whatever it is, I am against it" or, as I put it, "I'll do anything as long as it's against."

If, like most parents, you have these two kinds of children, then you will find that the Agreeables will probably accept your values and the Espiritus won't—at least not right away. When I pointed anything out to the Agreeables, they would say, "You think that?" and go off to ponder the matter. Then they'd return and say, "I've been thinking over what you said and I think you're right/wrong because...."

With the Espiritus, I felt that the minute the sound of my voice hit their ears, their mouths automatically opened to express opposition. What I said didn't enter their brains and certainly wasn't given much thought. Yet they must have stored it somewhere because ten years later they uphold a value they rejected in their teens. Espiritus tend to say, "I have to learn the hard way." I don't understand why, but I now say, "Be my guest."

It's said that a certain tribe of Indians never tell their little ones not to touch the fire in the tepee. They let the baby crawl to it then watch carefully so that he will not harm himself. After the baby touches the fire, he will never do it again until he is old enough to learn how to handle it.

Do you feel rejected personally when your children discard your values? I did. Our values seem such an intrinsic part of who we are that in our minds they are rejecting us. That can be painful, especially when we don't sort out our essential values from the peripheral ones.

Lala was really upset when Jack let his hair grow long in the early seventies. We pointed out to her that he was doing well in school, worked with our church's youth group, had a job, and helped at home. If he could be all that, then surely he was entitled to let his hair grow, if that was his fancy. It was not unhealthy, illegal, or immoral.

Ten years later, Rob turns up with a punk haircut. I hit the ceiling. He couldn't understand why I was so upset since I thought his Mohawks were amusing. Mohawks seemed ethnic, but punk was something else.

"You see," I told him, "to me, punk is unwholesome and wholesomeness is a value for me."

"Hey, Ma," he countered, "am I wholesome?"

"Yes, you are."

"Then why should it bother you if I look unwholesome as long as I am wholesome?"

"Because I don't understand. If you are wholesome, why do you want to appear unwholesome?"

No answer.

Chip started sporting an earring. "How come you're wearing an earring, Chip?"

"It's to state that I'm not gay."

"Why? Is there a question that you might be? I'm not gay either but I don't have to go around saying I'm not."

Sometimes, short dialogues suffice. I don't know what I would have done if Rob had kept getting punk haircuts and Chip kept wearing the earring. Maybe we would have kept up a dialogue until one of us won the other over.

Actually, clothes, hairdos, and jewelry express peripheral values. It's part of the process where adolescents and young adults try on personalities for size in their search for their real selves. I'm fairly at ease about these things. Nonetheless, I was horrified when Chip came to Annie's wedding in a black turtleneck, black jacket, black and white plaid shorts, no socks, and loafers. His comment? "Ann said it's okay."

It begins to hit hard when our central values are challenged. Charity is one. Are they kind, thoughtful, caring, giving? Do they care about the plight of the poor, the aged, the handicapped, the suffering? Faith is another. Are they faithful to God? Have they left the Church? Chastity. Who believes in chastity anymore? This covers premarital sex, living together before marriage, unwed pregnancies, abortion. Integrity. Are they honest? Do they cheat and lie? Education. Do they opt not to go to college or even drop out of high school? Family. Do they choose to absent themselves from family gatherings? Maybe they refuse to have anything to do with the family. Health. Do they indulge in substance abuse or blatantly abuse their health? These are the blockbusters and it's only a start.

The best and the most we can do is to inculcate them with our values and live out these values ourselves. It's pointless to insist that our children serve others when we don't do that ourselves. It doesn't work either when we serve our children, hoping to set a good example if we don't invite them to serve others. They might think it is their rightful due to be served.

It's important to support our values with reasons. Often these values originated generations before us and we haven't questioned them nor discovered the reasons behind them.

The story is told about the bride who was preparing her first roast beef dinner. She cut off a piece of the roast before she placed both pieces in the pan. Her husband asked her why she did this and she replied that her mother did it that way. The next time he saw his mother-in-law, the young man asked her the same question. "Mother did it that way," she said. More curious than ever, the young man asked his grandmother-in-law. She said, "I didn't have a pan big enough to hold the entire roast without cutting off a piece first."

In this process of finding reasons for my values, I had several things going for me: 1) Many different people raised me so I chose the values I wanted to keep and considered the reasons why. 2) I read a lot. 3) Incredibly wonderful people touched my heart, my mind, and my life. 4) Lala made me explain my decisions for whatever I did with our children. That last one alone is enough for anyone to have reasons for every value she tries to live by!

When I first met Mary Reed Newland, the writer, we were entering the "teen scene." Chrissy was fourteen; Bim was thirteen. Mary said, "If you think the teen years are difficult, wait till they become young adults!" We couldn't understand how that could be worse. Then they became young adults.

In childhood, they test their limits. As teenagers, they rebel and kick against the goad. But in young adulthood, they carry out their options: forego college, marry before they are ready, take a dubious job, refuse to work and lie around the house, assume an objectionable life-style.

We faced a major family crisis and I felt responsible for it. Had I been a better mother, perhaps it wouldn't have happened. Bim said, "Why do you feel responsible, Mom? We are free. God does not count himself responsible for the choices we freely make. Why do you? Are you bigger than God?"

And that is the bottom line—our children are free. All we can do is love them, pray for them, trust that Jesus is Lord and that "to them that love God, all things work together unto good."

Thank you, Lala!

CHAPTER XXIII

"AS YOU LIE THERE IN SMITHEREENS"—LETTING GO

"The choices we freely make." Sometimes I wish there were no free will. Life would be much simpler. Can you imagine what life would be like if the sun rose and set when it chose, depending on its mood?

My students invariably ask, "Why did God make free will? It just causes all sorts of problems!"

"Suppose," I answer, "you wanted a boyfriend. You go to an android store, order one built to your specifications: the height, weight, build, hair color you want. You choose the color of his eyes, the shape of his nose; every feature is handpicked. You get to decide whether his hair will be straight, wavy, or curly. You take him home and program him just as you want him: athletic, brainy, good dancer, hardworking, quiet, sensitive, maybe aggressive and macho. You choose. You program his personality and the things he'll say to you. You also program his responses to you. He is exactly as you want a man to be; you programmed him. Wouldn't that be awesome?"

"No, because I programmed him. He isn't really anyone. He isn't expressing himself. There is no himself."

"That's why God made free will."

"But we don't always choose him."

"That's the chance he took and that is precisely the problem. We do not choose him."

Tom had just graduated from high school and announced that he wasn't going to college. That upset Papa. Tom couldn't understand this. Why was Papa so upset by this?

"Tom, Papa is this kind of parent. If he sees his son standing on the edge of a cliff preparing to jump, he will pull him away from the edge, stand before him with arms outstretched, and say, 'I won't let you.' "

"What kind are you? You're not that upset."

"I'm the kind who'll say, 'Son, if you jump, you'll lie in smithereens at the bottom.' Then, when you lie there in smithereens, you'll say, 'By golly, she was right!' My theme song, if you haven't noticed, is 'Nanny, nanny booboo!' "

Recounting this story to some friends, one of them said, "But you'd pick up the pieces. Right?"

"Nope."

If someone ran him off the cliff or if he fell in the darkness, I would. But if he deliberately jumped, knowing what he was doing, then we're back to "In life, there are neither rewards nor punishments, only consequences." I mentioned earlier that we don't believe in bailing out. When you know there will be no one to pick up the smithereens, you will be less likely to jump. At least, you will think about it.

Time improves perspective. In Mary's case, she realized that not going to college was a disadvantage. At the prompting of our cousins, Nil and Lyn, she decided to give it a try on the other side of the world—in the Philippines. We salute her for this valiant effort. There is much to be said for someone who understands she took the wrong path, backtracks, and goes running down the happy path. More power to her!

When the second of our brood ventured into adolescence, she insisted on trying her wings. We were overprotective since we had grown up in a culture that is protective of its young. The more overprotective we got, the harder she fought us. Finally I understood that adolescence is the bridge between childhood and maturity. It isn't wide but it's fairly long. We are so afraid that our "little ones" will fall into the water. Many of us, then, try to hold their arms as they walk across. They struggle so hard to be free of our hold that they often end up falling into the water, taking us with them. If we had waited for them on the maturity side, they would be careful not to fall, and they'd walk right down the middle of the bridge with great care. In the meantime, we could encourage and cheer them on.

I believe we have only nine months and twelve years to get our licks in. To get anything in after that is generally a lost cause because anything after twelve is too late. When they enter their teen years, we need to start bowing out and turning the reins of their lives over to them. The arrangement we made with our children was an even exchange: "Deliver the maturity and we'll turn over the freedom."

We're overprotective because we're afraid our children will make mistakes they'll pay for the rest of their lives. Joe wanted to get married much earlier than we preferred. We voiced our reservations and he said, "I am prepared to assume the responsibilities that will be the consequences of my decision."

"I'm so glad," I said, "because we are not going to."

He was true to his word. Before the year was out, he was manager of his store and his wife, Theresa, graduated cum laude from nursing school. They now have four bright, lively kids. The thing I like most about Joe and Theresa's marriage is their ability to laugh together a lot.

I am surprised when parents dictate to their kids the courses to choose in school. Our kids chose their colleges, their majors, and their courses. They also put themselves through college. We are proud of all they have achieved of their own free will and effort.

We fear our children's mistakes because they seem to reflect on us as parents. We measure our worth as parents by the successes of our children. To some parents, success means having a son graduate from Harvard with a medical degree or a daughter who earns $80,000 as a corporate lawyer. To other parents, it's having a priest son or happily married children. We have our own definitions of parent success.

When one of our children made an unfortunate decision, we were devastated. Fr. Bob asked us, "What is God saying to you in this?"

"Well, you sure aren't as hot a mother as you hoped you'd be, are you?"

"God doesn't talk like that, you know."

"So tell me, Father."

"He is saying you must not measure your worth by what your children do."

Then there are dreams. We dream dreams for our children just like our parents dreamed dreams for us. Knowing that, I try not to dream for mine. Nevertheless, we do it without thinking. After we went to Bishop Alvaro Corrada's ordination as bishop, I thought how nice it would be if Rob could be a bishop. Bishop Corrada, I believe, is also the youngest of a large family. I told Rob this.

"Mom!" he spluttered. "I have plans."

"I know, Dear. So I told God all I really wanted was that you become a saint."

"Now," he said, calming down, "that's okay."

In the final analysis, letting go is a matter of trust. Trust God to be Lord of our lives and those of our children; trust that our children are, at least, as good as we are; trust that our love for them will be equal to whatever life has in store.

Letting go is freeing. It frees the Lord to be Lord because we're not running interference anymore. It frees our children to be themselves. It frees us from the need to be in control and from anxiety, worry, and handwringing.

We seem to return to Bim's comment, "Mom, we are free!" But she didn't end there. She went on to say, "Mom, a good family isn't one where no one makes mistakes. A good family makes mistakes but continues to love and forgive each other, uphold and be there for each other."

Thanks again, Bim! We're proud of you, Mary!
Thank you, Nil and Lyn!

CHAPTER XXIV

MY LEGACY

Lala grew up on a little farm in Missouri, so poor they had eggs only at Easter. Most of the time, only their father ate meat because he worked the hardest. Lolo grew up in a fishing village in Negros in the Philippines. With much effort and unflagging determination, Lala became a graduate nurse and Lolo, a physician. They managed to send Papa to Georgetown University. Being poor did not deter them from making their dreams come true.

Born to landowners, I had a comfortable childhood. It didn't take me long to recognize that happiness had little to do with possessions. Anita belonged to one of Manila's richest families. She had her own apartment, her own car from her parents, and a hefty allowance. Nevertheless, she was one of the most discontented people I'd ever met. By contrast, Estelita had lost an eye, an arm, and a leg during the war, but she had a merrier heart. Conclusion: circumstances do not determine joy.

You know how in your heart of hearts you want to be the best at something—anything at all? I did. But there was always someone prettier, smarter, kinder than I. Finally, I found two spaces I could occupy: (1) No one needed God more than I and (2) I was going to become the happiest person I know. First, I had to learn how to be happy.

I already knew that circumstances did not determine joy. I learned from Abraham Lincoln that "Folks are as happy as they make up their minds to be." I remember waking up many mornings knowing I had to face a couple of babies in diapers, get five kids off to school, launder six tubs of clothes. But I'd grit my teeth and think, "By gum, I'm going to be happy today if it kills me!" I recalled this little old lady's advice to the little girl, "Life is tough but it's got to be lived, so stick a daisy in your hat and be happy!"

In college I read Thoreau and took his words to heart:

> I went to the woods because I wished to live life deliberately, to front only the essential facts of life, and see if I could not learn what it had to teach, and not, when I came to die, discover that I had not lived. I did not wish to live what was not life, living is so dear; nor did I wish to practice resignation, unless it was quite necessary. I wanted to live deep and suck out all the marrow of life....

I concluded it was not possible to be truly happy unless I lived what was truly life. Therefore, I had to focus on the "essential facts of life."

Finally, I met St. Francis and his notion of perfect joy. Very briefly, it goes something like this. He said that if he and the friars went home and found a warm welcome, a warm dinner, and warm beds, it would not be perfect joy; it would be logic. If they went home to a warm welcome, a warm dinner, and cold beds, there would still be logical causes for joy. If they went home to a warm welcome, a cold dinner, and cold beds, there was still one logical reason to be joyful. But if they got home and the friars scolded them, refused to give them food, and threw them out in the snow for the night and they still managed to be joyful, that is perfect joy!

These were the foundations of my philosophy of joy. The fact that our material resources were fairly limited was another major foundation. This led us to look for and discover the many ways of having frugal fun.

That's the reason we took to camping in 1957. The first time we went, we left town with two dollars, both of us thinking the other had more money. When we returned, we had one dollar. Can you beat that for frugality?

We often waited until drive-ins had their two dollar per carload specials. Back then, drive-in movies showed family movies. We recall another favorite memory. We bought a kite for a dollar and a half at People's Drug Store, packed a picnic dinner, and went to the Marian novitiate backfields to fly the kite. The Marians welcomed us royally.

This led to a different orientation in just about everything. When we needed a new roof, we all got on the roof to rip off the old shingles. Then our two house-builders, Bob and Tom, supervised our putting on the new roof. When Bim and Bob were expecting Jeremiah, their friends, our Team of Our Lady, and our Bible study group turned up and in Amish fashion built an addition to their little cabin in one day.

Today, our children, with their ingenuity, continue to foster family fun. They avail themselves of the many services our libraries provide. They can take out videos from the library for less than the charge at video stores. Our park system and the zoo are excellent—both for free!

Our weddings are "homemade"—and personal. Chrissy caters the reception with her friends, Deedee and Natalie. Nini and I help with the food. Bim makes the flower arrangements. Mecky does the sewing, Jack and Tom furnish the music, and Joe is the photographer. Ann and Mary sing.

When Lala died, we had her wake at home and the grandchildren witnessed first hand how death is very much a part of life.

When he was a child, Dick Gregory's mother told him, "We are not poor, just broke." And that's how it was for us. We were broke but wealthy in all the things that really count. We didn't have many things that most people take for granted but, somehow, that didn't matter.

We have much going for us. Early in our marriage we heard of a French Canadian custom, I believe it was, of putting one's bills under the statue of the Infant Jesus of Prague, a visible sign that he is king of our household and of all our needs. He has stood by us over the years. The Boy Scouts told us they could tell when we were particularly broke: Baby Jesus was unusually tall. We keep important things under him, too. It puzzles people when someone asks, "Mom, where's the check that came in the mail for me?" and I answer "It's under Baby Jesus."

Another custom we read about suggested giving to the Lord whatever you have when you are really broke. Luke 6:38 says, "If you give, you will get! Your gift will return to you in full and overflowing measure, pressed down, shaken together to make room for more, and running over. Whatever measure you use to give—large or small—will be used to measure what is given back to you." The Lord is never outdone.

Divine Providence always provides. As Philippians 4:19 points out: "It is God who will supply all your needs from his riches in glory, because of what Christ Jesus has done for us." Though he has chosen not to give us material wealth of our own, he has gifted us with relatives and friends who lovingly share their material abundance with us. We can never repay them for all they have done for us. Only God can. Our life truly proves there is a provident, loving God.

As children, ours often came to us and said, "This friend has this and that friend has that. We kinda wish we had such things, too." Many of my friends express guilt because they can't provide their children with the things their friends possess. I simply said to my kids, "The legacy I hope to leave you is not worldly goods but the ability to be happy without depending on anything outside yourselves."

The title of John Powell's book says it all: *Happiness is an inside job*.

Thank you so much, Abundance sharers!

CHAPTER XXV

THE TWAIN SHALL MEET

Was it Kipling who wrote, "East is East and West is West, and never the twain shall meet"? But it has in us.

There is a decided advantage in operating from and in more than one culture. Emilia, however, didn't agree. She felt she wasn't doing the correct thing in this culture. I experienced the contrary; I found it freeing. When I didn't do things quite right, others were quick to excuse me because I came from another country.

The nicest thing about being multicultural is that we can pick and choose the best of our several worlds. I say "multi" instead of "bi" because many cultures feed into the Filipino one. Our aborigines were black pygmies. We were under Spain for almost four centuries. Our educational system after that was American and because we have so many different languages, our common language is English. The Chinese have lived among us since time immemorial, and we have the same racial roots as the Indonesians and the Malayans. In effect, we are English-speaking, Hispanic Orientals.

We see life and the world from the viewpoints of Americans, Hispanics, and Orientals. Because of this, we realize quite well that there is no absolute way of being. What is acceptable in one culture can be taboo in another, and vice versa. We are not locked into one set of rights and wrongs because most things in life are relative. Very few things are earthshaking. I can think of only two absolutes: God and love. St. John says they're the same. As we went along, we chose those traits from our different cultures that we wanted in our lives.

When Chrissy read the first draft of my opening chapters, she said, "I think you've missed the whole point, Mom. This entire thing about enjoying children is cultural. Filipinos believe children are for enjoying—truly gifts from God. The life-style of the whole country supports that: extended family and domestic help."

Family is a strong value in Philippine culture. Family ties are nurtured and kept close for generations. My fifth cousins and I still call each other "cousin." I find it astounding that some first cousins here in the United States don't see each other for years even when they live in the same town. When we were children in the Philippines, first cousins frequently gathered on Sunday after Mass at the Big House—Grandpa and Grandma's. I was equally astounded that this is changing fast; when we recently went back for a visit, my first cousins' children were meeting each other for the first time at a party for us. Signs of the times, but my hope is that our grandchildren's children will be as close to each other as their parents are.

However, the Filipino family system fosters dependence among their young because it seems easier to control those dependent on you. They tend to live at home until they marry or enter religious life. If they do neither, they just don't leave home. Independence was more attractive to us, but it often went counter to the value of strong family ties. So we fostered interdependence which combines self-sufficiency and family bonding. Our kids delivered papers, baby-sat, and got jobs at sixteen just like other All-American kids.

We liked the poise and openness of American kids and we valued Oriental respect for elders. We discovered they could co-exist in a child. We like the way Americans are organized and the easy-going, hang-loose ways of the Filipino. They could be combined! We admire the Americans' strong work ethic and love the Filipinos' propensity for celebration. So we work celebrating and celebrate working. These are just the obvious ones. We seem to combine automatically the elements we like and find that it allows us to have our cake and eat it too!

We don't stop there, either. We have a *mezzuzzah* on our front door and a Passover Seder every year. "You're not Jewish, are you?" people ask. We have *Pashka* and *Kulich* every Easter. "You're not Russian, are you?" We have *oplatek* on Christmas eve. "You're not Polish, are you?" We always have *Posadas* that night, too. "Are you Mexican?" I answer them all in the same way: "No, I just help myself to any ethnic custom I find meaningful."

In her book, *Traits of a Healthy Family,* Dolores Curran says that one of these traits is a "strong sense of family in which rituals and traditions abound." What are your family rituals and traditions? Joe wanted to know what we had that would be equivalent to the way the Africans lifted up their new babies to the moon as described in *Roots*. The closest we come to that are the little singing hand games and nonsense rhymes we do with our babies. Nothing is quite so heartwarming as listening to our children-in-law do these Visayan games with American accents: "Doo-rye, doo-rye, doo-rye, carabang, carabang, carabang."

Among the rituals and traditions we have developed over the years are the banners Chrissy makes for the baptism of every grandchild.

Phil used to say, "What I like about this family is that I can count on a fiesta every other week!" For some time, we celebrated every birthday. However, the girls have moved upstate and there are fifty-nine of us. Now, we select one day every month to celebrate all the birthdays for that month.

During Lent, we set up a cross that Papa made with two purple candles at its base. On Easter morning, we drape the white cloth on it, change the candles to white, and place Easter flowers beside it. We don't mention the Easter bunny. On the Fourth of July, we celebrate Nini's, Lizzy's, Mary's, and Connor's birthdays. At Christmas we take a family picture that goes into "Jubilation," our seasonal family letter. We celebrate Halloween and Thanksgiving in a special way, too.

There were others that were fun celebrations, but situations have changed and keeping all the traditions became a hardship. We had to give some of them up. At one time there was Lala's apple butter gettogether in October, a re-living of her childhood when we made nine to eighteen bushels of apples into apple-butter in a copper kettle over a wood fire, stirring it with a wooden paddle. After she died, we stopped doing it. None of us really liked apple butter enough to go to all that trouble. We did it because she loved it!

We've shelved our St. Nicholas Puppet Show on December 6. Wanting our children to realize that St. Nicholas was not Christmas, we would celebrate his feast with a puppet show where St. Nicholas himself explained that Christmas is about the Baby Jesus. We did this for at least twenty years! The puppets were homemade and Bim and Jack were our star puppeteers. Everyone else took turns.

Another obsolete custom was our trek to the woods to gather crowfeet for Advent wreaths. One year we even made hand-dipped candles. For about four years, we made incredible amounts of pisseles.

Advent is a great time for family rituals and traditions. The Krist Kindl game is my favorite; it seems to be played everywhere. You probably know it as "Kris Kringle," where each person buys a gift for his/her KK. The Krist Kindl game is not quite the same. You draw the name of your Krist Kindl from a hat and treat this person all Advent long as if he or she were the Christ Child. (Krist Kindl means Christ Child.) In our family, that meant being especially kind and patient to your KKs, doing extra things for them such as making their bed, putting away their clean clothes—this kind of thing. "But, Mom," Bim said, "if Jack sees me making his bed, he'll know he's my KK." "Then make Tom's and Joe's too. That'll confuse all of them."

The highlight of the year is the Posadas. This is a reenactmemt of Joseph and Mary's search for room at any inn in Bethlehem. In Mexico, this is done among the homes in a village or neighborhood. For us, the bedrooms, the upstairs bathroom, and the kitchen are the inns. The family gathers on Christmas Eve at six o'clock for Christmas dinner. At 7:30 we announce Posadas time and all innkeepers scramble to their inns.

If a couple is expecting a baby that year, they are Mary and Joseph. If not, the grandchildren draw lots for the roles. They carry the creche figurines of Mary and Joseph, the donkey, the shepherds and sheep, and the angel. At eight we start up the stairs singing "Come, all ye faithful." We stop before a door and Joseph knocks to ask for a room. With each year, the innkeepers become funnier, crazier, and more outrageous. Bob and Phil try to outdo each other. When we reach the kitchen door, the last innkeeper leads Mary and Joseph to the empty stable where we place all the figurines. Papa reads the Christmas Gospel, Jack reads *'Twas the Night Before Christmas,* and we sing Christmas carols.

When we return from Midnight Mass, we sing "Happy Birthday" to our newborn God and there is a birthday cake. When Rob was nearly four, he asked, "When are we going to shoot the cake?"

"Shoot the cake?"

"Yes, so it'll die and go to heaven and Jesus can eat it."

We call all of this "creating memories." We are all for it! We believe in photographs; our two shelves of albums attest to that. We tape the children singing and reciting poems. Jack was such an accident-prone child that every time he'd have an accident I'd say, "If you reach twenty-one alive and whole, I'll ring the bells at St.

John's." Ring them I did. Papa taped the whole thing newscaster style, complete with interviews.

A month after Papa's close call with death when he had a craniotomy, we held a family conference to share our feelings. One thing came up repeatedly. Our children wanted their children to have memories of Papa doing things with them: camping, learning to tie knots, fishing, hunting, planting things, singing songs. Since then, Papa has deliberately "created memories" with the little ones. He commented after one such deliberate effort that "camping with five grandchildren at sixty-four isn't like camping with eleven twenty years ago! Next time, you come along!"

Do you tell family stories to your children? I loved hearing family stories as a child and I pass them on to our children and grandchildren. Nanay's stories gave me a warm inner glow. The scenes of her childhood that she created for me are still as vivid as they were when I sat on her lap. Lala, too, was quite a storyteller. When she was in her nineties, we captured her stories on tape. The grandchildren love to hear over and over again the stories about their parents. This gives children a deeper sense of who they are. Every in-law, too, brings in a whole new vein of family stories that greatly increase the wealth of an already incredible treasure trove.

The French call their in-laws "beautiful whatever." Father-in-law, for example is beau père—handsome father. The Chinese consider every relative of an in-law their relative too. By that reckoning, we are related to all the relatives of our beautiful children. Talk about rich!

The author of my opening quote is, indeed, Rudyard Kipling. The poem goes like this:

> Oh, East is East and West is West,
> and never the twain shall meet,
> Till Earth and Sky stand presently
> at God's great Judgment Seat;
> But there is neither East nor West,
> border, nor breed, nor birth,
> When two strong men stand face to face,
> though they come from the ends of the earth!

For *two strong men,* read *loving people.* It is the truth.

Thank you, Krist Kindls and innkeepers!

CHAPTER XXVI

"ARE YOU MY FRIEND?"

I frequently ask the little children in my life this question: "Are you my friend?" I ask it without thinking, wanting to know whether these children whom I often intimidate think of me as friend or foe.

When Bim was younger and wanted her way about something, I said to her, "Listen, there is room for only one SOB in this family, and that's me," hitting myself on the chest with great vigor to make my point. "If you want the position, you'll have to fight for it because I'm not relinquishing it willingly. When I am kind, patient, understanding and all that, you all turn into brats. So better one SOB and eleven wonderful people than one wonderful mother and eleven brats! You wanna fight?" Do you see why I frequently ask that question?

When Bim was twenty-one, she gave me an answer. I had taken care of a woman in our parish who was very sick and could barely function. She had had seven children in stair-step fashion; the oldest was thirteen. The children made incredible demands on her. As she lay on the couch, barely able to move, they'd come in one by one and ask her to tie their shoes, get them a drink of water, make sandwiches—all things they could do for themselves. I finally got them to stop such demands by threatening to take them home with me!

When I got home, I looked for my children. The only one I could find was Bim, holed up in her room in the attic. "I just took care of these kids. Now I understand for the first time why people rave about how good you guys are. So I want to thank you for being so good. I never really appreciated you enough."

"D'you know why we were so good?"

"Why?"

"Because you were such a b___ch!" And she meant that as a compliment.

When I ask, "Are you my friend?" the answer I get is a smiling "Yes." I have a hunch that my "beautiful children and grandchildren" consider me a friend because they like to come and chit-chat. They seem to have no trouble talking with me about anything and everything. But I can't claim I am their friend. They must do that.

I can claim that they definitely are *my* friends. I often hear parents say they don't want to be their children's friend. "I'm his father, not his pal." I think they mean they are there to give love and discipline, but not goof around with their kids. I agree totally. A verduga is not someone that kids goof around with. However, I also believe that friendship is much more than goofing around.

Paul Hinnebusch's definition says "Friendship is two lives joined in love and lived as one." Friendship is an affinity of two spirits who greatly enjoy each other and seek each other out because they complete each other. I have a tremendous affinity for the spirits of my family members, greatly enjoy them, and seek them out because they fulfill and complete me. What they have done over the years is to call forth the best from me, hone away my selfishness, and invite me to be the most loving person I know how to be.

In his book, *From Beirut to Jerusalem,* Thomas L. Friedman says "Only a real friend tells you the truth about yourself." I paraphrase what he says: "A friend helps to jar us out of our fantasies by constantly holding up before our eyes the mirror of reality."

Friends allow us to look into the mirror without fear because we know they have seen our reality and continue to love us anyway. The message I hope I have given my children is not "Be this so I can love you," but rather, "I love you so much; you can be everything you choose to be!" In truth, this is the message they have given me.

After twenty-five chapters, I cannot tell you why our children are such appreciative people. Mecky always speaks about how much she owes us for all we have done for her. I don't know what those are. She is the one who does all sorts of things for others.

I have been giving pointers on "how-to" with children. In reality, I have learned more from them than they have from me. They were born with wisdom I struggle for and acquire only piecemeal year after year. My wisdom lies in recognizing wisdom in others. I watch my children in action—and I learn. I follow their example. They are incredible role models.

They are also my psychiatrists. My sister Ging once said, "A psychiatrist is just a surrogate friend." I learned what compassion and healing meant from Jack. It was our twenty-fifth wedding anniversary and I was upset with Papa for something he had done. Jack found me crying while I folded clothes in the basement. He asked me if something was wrong and I proceeded to tell him how I felt. He pointed out that I had misread Papa's action, but I was beyond consoling. At this point, my twenty-one-year old son took me in his arms and wept with me. (Thank you, Jack!)

When Papa and I return from a vacation without the children, we might find the living room or the kitchen with a new coat of paint, the wood floors refinished, ceiling fans installed in the living room and kitchen, or new floors in the kitchen and bathroom. They are like that—ever giving.

I always told them we had so many of them because each one was so delightful that we wanted more. I told Rob he was the last because he was the perfect dessert!

When those Manila boys voted me the girl they least wanted to marry, I didn't dream anyone in his right mind would want to marry me, let alone that I would be the mother of eleven children. If I had to write the story of my life in one sentence, I could. I found this sentence written on the flyleaf of Elizabeth Barrett Browning's *Sonnets from the Portuguese* two weeks before I fell in love with Papa: "God's gifts put men's best dreams to shame!"

Actually, I can write the story of my life in one word: Alleluia!

Thank you, God!

CHAPTER XXVII

POSTSCRIPT

Jeanne Young, a longtime friend and Jack's "belle mère," called. During our conversation, she said she could see no real problems with our children. I couldn't let her go on with that illusion so I shared my realities with her. That is the reason for this postscript.

Our family enjoys getting together frequently, and we obviously have fun. Some of us are good at what we do. Because of this, people have a tendency to think we are a fancy family. In reality, we are as fancy as the next one. We are a very real family, not a storybook one.

Today, people refer to families as dysfunctional or functional. I go on record saying that our family is as dysfunctional as any other dysfunctional family. Name the dysfunction, and we've had it. What we have decided to do with our dysfunctions is what makes us functional.

When I fell in love with Papa, I was on such a high that I was forever singing. Nanay remarked, "I hope you will always be this happy."

I said, "I probably will be because I don't enjoy suffering."

"You silly child," she said, "as if suffering were a matter of enjoying or not enjoying!"

But I have found over the years that people who do not like to suffer go out of their way to prevent and minimize their suffering. They look for solutions to problems. They are open to suggested solutions and are willing to try them.

This is so logical that I often wonder why some people resist solutions. Perhaps it is because suffering is like being caught in a bramble bush. In time we learn that if we keep still, the thorns won't prick too much, but when we extricate ourselves from the bramble bush we get painful, bloody scratches and torn clothes.

In our family we either notice and remark that someone is caught in a bramble bush or we yell "Help!" We don't pretend everything is okay. In many good families, doing well is of prime importance. The members are achievers and winners; there are no losers or at least there had better not be losers. Joseph Kennedy said to his children, "Always come in first; second place is failure." Some people take great pains to make sure everything is okay and from all outward appearances everything really is okay.

We, however, are not one of those families. We believe you don't have to wear your girdle at home. The boys may call each other "winner," yet they are not afraid to admit their failures to us. When any one of us is trapped in a bramble bush, we either yell for help or call attention to the fact that someone needs it. Then we convene for a family conference so that the bramble-busher can open up and share. We truly listen and, hopefully, we help.

A month after Papa's close call with brain surgery, we felt a universal need to gather and share our feelings. Jack opened the discussion. "Mom, how do you feel about the fact that Dad is going to die?"

"You mean that he 'might' die."

"No; that he will die."

"Well, I always knew he wasn't immortal...."

"No, Mom, his dying has become a proximate reality."

We went from one to the other around the room. It began in a fairly controlled atmosphere. Soon, though, the tears came and the fears surfaced: "My children will have no memories of Papa." The regrets: "I have so much to make up to Papa; I have been such a dork to him for so long." The pain: "I will miss him so much; we are so close." The suffering and the love overflowed, the healing began, and the Spirit of God filled us once again.

I recall another major crisis when we hurled bitter words and unleashed a lot of anger. It was devastating. Jack, the family stabilizer, and Papa went out for a walk. Those of us who sat around the table wept. When Jack and Papa returned, Papa spoke from his heart the words that brought peace and love and strength. Then he turned and went to his room. "Don't leave him alone," Jack said. "Somebody go with him." Moments later, we all found Papa kneeling at the side of his bed, crying his heart out. Two of the children were there with their arms around him, doing the same. The rest of us joined them.

After a while, Jack said, "We haven't had singing prayers in a while. Before we turn in, let's sing 'Thank you, God,' like we used to." And holding hands, that's what we did.

Remembering this incident gives us the courage to approach the family when any one of us is in trouble. Having done this several times allows us to trust that the rest—including the beautiful children now—will come together as one body and support, accept, forgive, and cherish us.

Everyone seems to rush to the one enmeshed in the bramble bush, unhook each thorn gently, and extricate the "prisoner" with minimum scratches and tears. Love truly conquers all.

If this is true, then why is its application not universal? Perhaps because it takes time and energy. It takes effort and imagination. It means investing oneself. John Shea says, "It costs. It costs time, ingenuity, persistence, cleverness, clarity of purpose. It is easier to excommunicate and write them off."

When people cause us difficulty and pain, we find the quickest relief by avoiding them. It is typical today to deal with a problem by simply getting rid of its source. If having a baby is a problem, abort it. If your spouse causes you pain, leave him. If your children give you grief, kick them out. If your aging parents are burdensome, put them away. (I am not speaking here of situations where the nursing home is truly the only alternative, and the family keeps lavishing love and attention on their loved one.) Don't examine the problem and look for solutions; that's too complicated. Throw it away. Don't attack the problem head on. It's too messy so just dispose of it. This is the Disposable Age. Disposable hankies, disposable diapers, disposable pens, disposable people.

The person caught in the bramble bush knows this and fears to risk asking for help lest no one will answer. It is easier to sit very still. It is easier to continue dysfunctioning. Sometimes, healing takes courage because it means having to change.

When people know others love them, it bolsters their courage. Faith in that love assures them they will not be alone; there will be someone to hold them up when the going gets too rough; those who love them will walk through hell to bring them to heaven. TLC will buffer the fears; compassion and caring will assuage the pain.

Bim told us about an old, painful wound because she needed our support in order to be healed. Very simply, Chrissy said to her, "I now understand how Jesus could be willing to suffer for us because if I could, I would take on your pain just so you'd suffer less. That's how much I love you." Bim's courage in her self-revelation was awesome and the strength of Chrissy's love stunned me.

Then something unexpected happened. Someone else shared a deep, long-buried pain. So did another. And still another. They recognized what Bim had done—given us this enormous gift of trust by placing her pain in our hands. They wanted to give us the same gifts too. Such raw pain; so much raw courage. The outpouring of love was incredible!

Why, then, don't people take a chance? Responses similar to the foregoing are worth the risk. Maybe when things come apart in a family, there is the tendency to believe that this is the end. Our disposable mentality surfaces. When something is broken, don't fix it; throw it away. There was a time when people repaired broken things instead of throwing them away. We darned socks, glued plates together, rebound books, nailed furniture together. We mended things and kept them. Families are the same. We can mend—and keep—relationships.

The Spanish nuns who taught me to darn, darned so beautifully that it looked like embroidery. Today, when clothes have stains, we give them to Goodwill. When I got bad stains on my skirts, I'd give them to Annie. She'd paint flowers over them. When relationships get torn, it is time to darn the tears to look like embroidery. When stains mess up relationships, it's time to paint flowers.

In an effort to comfort me after a particularly painful family crisis when I was trying to make sense out of the broken shards, my sister Ging said, "Your special charism as a family is your ability to pick up the pieces and put them back together so that the bowl is as good and as strong and as beautiful as it was before. Usually the bowl is never quite the same after it is repaired, but your bowl is always good as new." Praise God!

It's said that when something broken is mended, it is stronger. That must be what makes our bowl so strong—all that glue! When Jack gave Confirmation retreats, he had the confirmands play "Will the real Holy Spirit please stand up?" The different "holy spirits" claimed to be "the strong, driving wind," "a tongue of fire," "a dove," "the glue that holds the community together." We know which one is the real Holy Spirit!

Here is another way of putting it. When the garbage hits the fan, gather it up and dump everything on the compost heap. Compost makes strawberries grow. As Papa said, "I cannot change what happened in the past however much I want to. I just want to be part of the healing now."

When all is said and done, the bottom line in being a life-giving family is this: strive to love as unconditionally as God loves us. Such love gives us the courage to say, "For all that has been, thanks. To all that shall be, yes!" We have enjoyed each other. We enjoy each other. We will always enjoy each other.

Where does such love come from? It begins when someone loves the others unconditionally and another wanting and willing to love the same way. It will go from there because love is catching. No human being has yet been born who can resist being loved. If you love someone strongly enough, long enough, the day will come when she or he will turn around and love you in return.

A loving family begins with you. Someone has already loved you unconditionally. God has.

Thank you, God!
Thank you, Jeanne Young!
Thank you, Ging!
Thank YOU!

EPILOGUE

Thou hast given me so much, O Lord,
Give one thing more, a grateful heart;
Not grateful when it pleaseth me,
As if thy blessings had fair days,
But such a one whose pulse might be
thy praise!

—George Herbert

www.ingramcontent.com/pod-product-compliance
Lightning Source LLC
Chambersburg PA
CBHW070915160426
43193CB00011B/1471